"As our lives become more digitized, the power of story-telling will rise, elevating our humanity. No one captures how to harness this tool as well as Murray Nossel. This is a fabulous handbook on how to connect through story-telling and how to listen with intent."

—FAITH POPCORN, founder and CEO of Faith Popcorn's Brain Reserve

"We are all overwhelmed by messages and content on various platforms, but what has not changed since our cavepeople predecessors is the importance and power of a great and compelling story. Stories are the key differentiator, and Murray Nossel's listening and storytelling methods provide a straightforward yet ingenious way to create that differentiation. Murray's method is the engine to foster the creativity and innovative thinking to tell a unique story. Powered by Storytelling is an indispensable asset."

—JONATHAN D. KLEIN, cofounder and chairman of Getty Images

"If you want to learn how to tell a great story, read this book. Murray Nossel, himself a psychologist and master storyteller whose own tales recall the best of David Sedaris, offers a unique method that is sure to work.

"Powered by Storytelling is much more than a how-to book about business communication. It's an important road map for anyone who wants to convey a point in a meeting, make a compelling argument to colleagues, and listen in a way that brings out the best stories in business and in life."

—SUSAN ADAMS, senior editor at *Forbes*

"*Murray Nossel presents a thoughtful guide, teaching us how to discover and tell the personal stories hiding within each of us—and he artfully illustrates how this brilliant tool can have a profound impact on group dynamics in any setting. If you're looking to spark new talent within your organization, this book generously reveals how you can be* Powered by Storytelling."

—ROB SORCHER, global chief content officer of Cartoon Network

"*Murray Nossel has forever changed my understanding of communication and deeply influenced my ability to communicate. His insights for the teller and the listener are simple yet profound.*"

—KATIA BEAUCHAMP, CEO of Birchbox

"*Murray Nossel's storytelling method acts like a laser beam in the hands of teachers and coaches. It pierces through the fog of the typical narrative to reveal the story-teller's sense of herself in the world. Bring this method to your work, and your students and clients will feel more in touch with themselves!"*

—MIKE G. KATZ, founding director of the Interpersonal Development Program at the University of California, Berkeley, Haas School of Business.

"We live in an age of white noise, a constant barrage of messaging, most of which is completely ignored. The only thing that cuts through is effective storytelling. Murray Nossel's Narativ method is a powerful, science-based, empathetic, and engaging process that enables anyone to excavate, craft, and present a story to form a deep connection with the listener."

—MARK RANDALL, assistant professor of strategic design and management at Parsons School of Design

"Psychologist, actor, and corporate consultant Murray Nossel brings Narativ's innovative practice of storytelling to the business community. Through a life lived onstage, in the academy, and in the boardroom, Nossel has discovered the enduring power of storytelling: one person describes an event in such sensory detail—what do I see, hear, taste, smell, touch?—that the listeners enter and experience the world of the teller. In his "What happened?" model, Nossel coaches his client groups toward empathy

for one another, trust for members of their team, and a shocking clarity for each storyteller. Powered by Storytelling *is a beacon for those in search of a workplace of collaboration, effective teamwork, authenticity, and joy.*

—RITA CHARON, MD, PHD, chair of the
Department of Medical Humanities and Ethics
at Columbia University

"In an era of increasingly loud echo chambers where genuine debate and dialogue are rarified, Powered by Storytelling *not only gives the reader a compelling method to create cohesion and express sentiment but also to generate listening behaviors that break through silos and truly transform business communication."*

—JIM KNIGHT, The Rt Hon Lord Knight of
Weymouth, Chief Education Adviser at TES
Global, and former Minister for Schools (U.K.)

"Murray Nossel teaches companies that better performance lies not only in better processes but in more empathetic processes, not only in more efficient meetings but in more aware meetings. Bringing our stories into work is what we do anyway—this book teaches us how to leverage their power."

—CRISTIAN LUPȘA, founding editor of
Decât o Revistă and founder of The Power
of Storytelling Conference

"We all have a story, but we don't all know how to tell it. This book will teach you. Inside Murray Nossel's sometimes hilarious, sometimes heartbreaking tales are the tools you need to craft your own narrative. I'm buying a copy for everyone I know. You should, too!"

—JANN TURNER, director on ABC's *Scandal* and NBC's *Chicago Fire*

Powered by
Storytelling

Powered by Storytelling

Excavate, Craft, and Present Stories to Transform Business Communication

Murray Nossel, PhD

Mc
Graw
Hill
Education

NEW YORK   CHICAGO   SAN FRANCISCO   ATHENS
LONDON   MADRID   MEXICO CITY   MILAN
NEW DELHI   SINGAPORE   SYDNEY   TORONTO

Except as permitted under the United States Copyright Act of 1976, no part of this publication may be reproduced or distributed in any form or by any means, or stored in a database or retrieval system, without the prior written permission of the publisher.

1 2 3 4 5 6 7 8 9   LCR   22 21 20 19 18

ISBN: 978-1-260-01190-6
MHID: 1-260-01190-9

e-ISBN: 978-1-260-01191-3
e-MHID: 1-260-01191-7

Design by Mauna Eichner and Lee Fukui

Library of Congress Cataloging-in-Publication Data

Names: Nossel, Murray, author.
Title: Powered by storytelling : excavate, craft, and present stories to
    transform business communication / Murray Nossel.
Description: New York : McGraw-Hill, [2018] l Includes index.
Identifiers: LCCN 2017055000l ISBN 9781260011906 (alk. paper)
    l ISBN
    1260011909
Subjects: LCSH: Communication in management. l Storytelling. l Business
    communication.
Classification: LCC HD30.3 .N67 2018 l DDC 658.4/5—dc23 LC record
available at https://lccn.loc.gov/2017055000

To David Hoos, my life partner

In memory of my father,
Norman Woolf Nossel (1932–2012),
a business visionary

CONTENTS

CONTENTS

PREFACE

....

M y career in transforming business communications using scientific methods began 30 years ago.
While I was completing my master's research in applied
psychology, my father asked me to travel to Bulawayo,
Zimbabwe, where his company had a pharmaceutical
factory.

Zimbabwe had recently undergone a political revolu-
tion in which the old white government led by Ian Smith
was replaced by the new black government of Robert
Mugabe. The ministers issued a decree that black employees move into the supervisory and managerial positions
that had been held mostly by whites since the factory
began production.

The factory director told me, "We've got a huge problem." Trained in the Rhodesian army, many of the white
managers had learned an authoritarian style and held
racist views. The black personnel had worked the ma-
chines and conveyor belts on the factory floor. They
hadn't been trained to lead. There was no way a white

man would accept a black man as his equal or boss. It was impossible.

My father was already working on a project to transform race relations in the South African workplace. He collaborated with a U.S.-based industrial psychologist, Dr. Melvin Sorcher, who specialized in behavioral change in the workplace. Sorcher's core belief was that racist attitudes were based on deep-rooted values and were difficult to change. However, Sorcher asserted that behavior was amenable to change. Over time, transformed behavior eventually would lead to shifts in values and attitudes. Focused on the ways people communicated, Sorcher developed a behavior modeling method to help people navigate conflict, resolve disagreements, and avoid emotional outbursts.

I trained in Sorcher's method and spent much of the year in Bulawayo applying his techniques. My process included videotaping actors role-playing conflict situations and screening those films with employees, who then took turns role-playing the situations in dyads. For example, in a module in which a supervisor was correcting a workplace behavior, the first step was always to acknowledge the supervisee for work he or she had done well. This step was based on studies showing that employees were more likely to listen to criticism after they'd been acknowledged.

The pharmaceutical company survived 47 years of political turmoil and continues to operate in Bulawayo. I would like to think that the behavior modeling work had something to do with its survival. Although my path to applying storytelling to business communication had not yet formally begun, this experience made a lasting impression on me. I understood that there are inventive ways to improve communication in business.

After Bulawayo I returned to South Africa to complete research I had begun on methods for improving creativity. Working in the laboratory at the Wits University Department of Applied Psychology, I used a pre-post test experimental design. First, I measured creativity. Then I exposed research participants to different procedures: sensory deprivation, brainstorming, and a control group. In brief, my study showed that brainstorming, in which one generates as many ideas as possible by freewheeling thought association and suspending judgment, had a positive impact on creativity. My conclusion was that the most effective way of enhancing creativity was learning how to suspend judgment. This observation would resurface to play a critical role in my listening and storytelling method.

After a two-year stint working in mental hospitals in Cape Town, I registered with the South African Medical and Dental Council as a clinical psychologist. Then I received my army call-up papers. After boot camp, I was appointed to the position of chief psychology officer of the Natal Medical Command. My patients were soldiers. Many had returned from months alone in the African bushveld with post-traumatic stress disorder (PTSD), vacant stares on their faces, and unable to speak.

Only one treatment worked. I asked them, "What happened?" and listened as they recounted tales of their encounters with enemy soldiers and wild animals. Whenever they got stuck in the telling, I'd ask, "What happened next?" It was then that I first witnessed the power of coupling storytelling with open, interested listening.

These experiences were like gathering kindling. The spark that lit the fire that would become the Narativ Method of Listening and Storytelling came through my experience as a social worker during the AIDS epidemic in New York City. The stories I gathered from AIDS patients became tools that put a human face on the epidemic when we presented them to legislators in Albany. Amid the urgency and tumult of that tragic period, I grasped that there was a reciprocal relationship between listening and storytelling. I also understood that stories functioned as living entities unto themselves; they were not static but were something more like a communication exchange between two parties, between listener and teller. In Chapter 1, you'll read the story of that moment during the AIDS epidemic. Telling that story is how I begin every training in transforming business communication.

Created during this urgent historical moment, when time was accelerated and choices were a matter of life and death, the Narativ Method of Listening and Storytelling has proved extraordinarily robust in settings with high demands and standards, notably business. Its ability to make audiences comfortable with the "human dimension" of work—all the thoughts, feelings, emotions, insight, and creativity that we often relegate to outside the office—continues to astonish and delight me. By reminding people of the reciprocal nature of all relationships, it paves a way for collaboration to deepen and communication to flourish.

I believe, and my method reveals, that we are all keen listeners and dynamic storytellers. We have stories to tell that pass on rich information about our jobs, our strategies, our conflicts and their resolutions, and our vision and the practical steps it takes for it to manifest. We have abilities in terms of listening and communicating that remain untapped and, once activated, will bring more fulfillment to our work by helping us unite our analytical abilities with our emotional intelligence.

In particular, when we bring the qualities of head and heart to teamwork, the result is closer collaboration, deeper bonds, and shared ownership. As you'll read throughout the book, cultural and social hurdles can be overcome through listening and storytelling. In many companies, I frequently encounter something that author Jon Katzenbach describes in his book *The Wisdom of Teams*: teams in which some members feel invisible, as if their ideas don't matter. As a result, they remain silent, and a great deal of knowledge is lost to the company, and productivity suffers.

Some of the most brilliant people I know are shy and reserved and have to be coaxed out of their inhibitions to speak. We need them to speak and contribute so that we obtain the best insight they have to offer. Storytelling ability is not normally a job requirement, but it can be cultivated. The Grandparent Exercise, for example, which we discuss in Chapter 4, is designed to ignite our presentational skills. I've yet to encounter any clients who, after participating in that exercise, don't leave with a fresh knowledge of the way they carry stories inside themselves and their natural ability to tell them.

I invite you to read and enjoy this book with a spirit of nonjudgment, the ethos of our method. Creativity and insight flow with nonjudgment. Empathy and understanding depend on it. Collaboration accrues in an environment of appreciation rather than criticism. Please take our method, developed over 25 years in thousands of person-to-person and group settings, and revolutionize your own approach to communication, as well as that of your team. The results will be nothing less than transformative.

ACKNOWLEDGMENTS

....

I would like to thank the innumerable teachers, students, clients, doctors, artistic collaborators, family members, and friends who've directly and indirectly contributed to *Powered by Storytelling* and the listening and storytelling method it presents.

In particular, I've been graced to work with patients who placed their trust in the method and in me even when many were at death's doorstep.

I would like to acknowledge my teacher Dzigar Kongtrul Rinpoche for teaching me how to listen to myself and others with an open heart and rigorous analytical mind.

Thanks to the late Ed Victor, through whom I had the great fortune to meet my agent, William Clark. William is instrumental in the book's existence. He had the wisdom and skill to understand my intentions. His confidence, support, focus, and encouragement endured through multiple iterations.

Casey Ebro, my editor at McGraw-Hill, read an article about Narativ in the *New York Times*. Her crystal-clear vision of a book using the listening and storytelling method to transform business communication is the impetus for what you are reading now. Her faith in me survived a somewhat florid first draft. Her subsequent congratulations were among the sweetest words I've ever heard. I am also grateful for the interest and support of Donya Dickerson, editorial director at McGraw-Hill, and for the expert assistance of Cheryl Ringer and Amy Li.

When I received Casey's substantive notes on my first manuscript draft, I turned to my business partners, Jerome Deroy and Sasha Meyerowitz, and said, "Help. I can't do this alone." Over the next two months, Jerome, Sasha, and I dismantled the manuscript. They asked questions, prodded me to tell stories, and pored through hundreds of documents. Jerome meticulously revisited his own experiences teaching Narativ's method in business. Sasha is a gifted editor and writer. I will never forget those days, and I will always cherish the camaraderie and fellowship that come with wanting to do the best work possible. That is the essence of partnership.

In 1974, in Johannesburg, South Africa, a teacher taught a class of ninth graders an exercise: turn to the person next to you and tell each other a story. Paul Browde and I were partners in that exercise. He told me a story, and then he asked me, "What's your story, Murray?"

I said I didn't have one. After that, we parted ways. Nearly 20 years later, Paul and I met unexpectedly in New York City. He was a psychiatrist in training, and I was an aspiring playwright. Miraculously, I had a second chance to tell him my story. The back-and-forth of listening and telling between us formed the backbone of the listening and storytelling method, and it provided the impetus for us to create Narativ Inc. and the performance piece *Two Men Talking*. We have traveled a long road together, and continue to do so. I want to express my gratitude to Paul for his friendship, encouragement, wisdom, and partnership.

Kimberley Bonnell worked from transcripts of my seminars and master classes to provide the first written synthesis of the method and the first workbook. John Glassie helped me with my first proposal. Harriet Bell pored over thousands of pages, going beyond the call of duty to "climb into my head" and reflect what she saw. Hopefully, she made it out unharmed.

Thanks to Marcelo Guidoli for bringing intelligence and flair to the book's illustrations.

A dedicated team leads Narativ workshops around the world. I have learned so much from the experience, wisdom, and skill of Jane Nash and Benaifer Bhadha. Dan Milne has taught me everything I know about performance.

Alana Dave's vision and support were seminal in applying Narativ's methods to large-scale social problems.

Cynthia Eyakuze, Brett Davidson, and Katarzyna Pabijanek from the Open Society Foundations have afforded me the opportunity to adapt the listening and storytelling method to a diverse international community of social justice advocates. Likewise, the staff and students of Columbia University's Department of Narrative Medicine have contributed to the evolution of the method.

For being an ardent supporter of Narativ's methodology and for connecting me with businesses wherever she could, I'd like to thank Trisha Coburn.

I would also like to thank Susan Calhoun, Barbara Adair, Terence Mickey, Dr. Harold Kimmel, Adrian Gore, Craig Kostelic, Victoria Kussman, Sean Nossel, Sally Smith, Lew Rubin, and Professor Barbara Hahn for their close readings of my drafts and invaluable suggestions.

Olga Tsyganova, Liza Wilcox, and Richard McLachlan provided superb research support. Professor Mindy Fullilove has been enormously generous in sharing her applications of Narativ's method.

For reflecting on my ideas about transforming business communications, I'd like to thank Bob Fitzpatrick, Ted Coburn, David Dowd, Steven Miller, Jullien Gordon, Roger Zionst, Kristian Klouda, Miranda Harper, Lance Schaffer, Lorna Bains, Russ Charlton, Steven Fiedler, Tony Latino, Art de Maesschalck, and Dr. Jun Su.

To the host of friends, family, and supporters circling around, encouraging me, and keeping it real, I have the greatest appreciation: Dr. Roger Babb, Kate Bednarski, John Burt, Heather Cariou, Gail Catlin, Thea and Jeff Chandross, Trace Cohen, Wendy Conquest, Dr. Jeremy Coplan, Willem de Vries, Dr. Simon Fortin, Natalie Gamsu, Dr. Daryl Glaser, Shirley Glaser, Dr. Edward Goldberg, Monika Gross, Clive Helfet, Brett Harwood, Craig Harwood, Leslie Harwood, Lowell Harwood, Professor Craig Irvine, Belinda, Barry, and Mia Kussman, Dr. Pierre Laramee, the Mangala Shri Bhuti community, Eddie Marritz, Hana Mahotka, Dr. Max McDowell, Tim Messler, Megan, Aaron, Benjamin, and Gideon Metrikin, Anton Meyerowitz, Tajana Meyerowitz, Philip Miller, Charlie Moss, Nadiya Nottingham, Lynn Philips, Dr. Richard Raskin, Friedrich Rosenfeld, Doug Safranek, Tim Saternow, Don Shewey, Becca Solow, Ashley Smith, Professor Maura Spiegel, Dewi Tan, Linda van Schaick, Alex van Schaick, and Patricia van Heerden, Kai Margarida-Ramirez, and Mateo Sky Deroy.

In the nonhuman realm, our cat, Lulubelle, has been my constant companion and is one of the best listeners ever.

Last, I would like to express my appreciation for my mother, Pauline Nossel, a brilliant musician, who taught me how to listen to myself and others for what is genuine, true, and beautiful. She is exacting and tireless. After years of dodging her questions about the book's progress, I'm ecstatic to tell her that it's done.

Powered by
Storytelling

INTRODUCTION

....

Tibetan Buddhist monks excel at concentration. They tell a traditional tale about focus called "The Lion's Gaze":

> When you throw a ball to a dog, it chases the ball. But when you throw a ball to a lion, it keeps its gaze on you.

When we tell a story, our Lion's Gaze is on one thing: connecting with our audience. In this book, my gaze is to connect with you, the reader, about how to use storytelling effectively in business communication. If I were at a sales meeting, my gaze would be to connect with the other sales reps about the sale that changed my life. A leader's gaze is to connect with his or her management team through a story about why the business exists. Connection is where the transformation of business communication happens. In other words, the effectiveness of your communication is commensurate with the depth

1

of your connection. And nothing makes that connection better than the story you tell.

In the Narativ method, we create stories in three phases:

1. **Excavating:** Generating your story ideas

2. **Crafting:** Shaping your story elements into a classic story structure

3. **Presenting:** Performing your story for an audience

By the end of this book, you will have a much better understanding of how to excavate, craft, and present a story. Stories don't live in a vacuum, however, and while you're learning about storytelling, you'll also be introduced to a larger framework of communication analysis into which stories are set. This heuristic relies on (1) science and (2) empirical evidence gathered over 25 years of research and practice in listening and storytelling.

BASIC PRINCIPLES OF THE NARATIV METHOD

To tell stories successfully, we need to understand a little about why stories connect and a lot about how to build that connection through listening and storytelling. It's important for me to emphasize that in our method, listening is of equal importance to telling, if not more so. We'll explore that idea in depth in Chapter 2. Let's begin by looking at the basic principles of our method:

1. Humans are hardwired for story.

2. Everyone has a story.

3. Everyone can learn to tell his or her story better.

4. Everyone's story will evolve.

5. Storytelling is every person's access to creativity.

6. There is a reciprocal relationship between listening and telling.

Principle 1. Humans Are Hardwired for Story

During a recent trip back to South Africa, I interviewed the paleoanthropologist Professor Phillip Tobias. Collaborating with Louis Leakey in the 1960s, Tobias identified, described, and named a new species: *Homo habilis*.[1] I asked him how far back in human history storytelling might go. I was aware of the Chauvet cave paintings, thought to be over 30,000 years old, in southeastern France and their images of rhinoceroses, cats, and bears. To me, this seemed like evidence of early storytelling.

"My dear," Professor Tobias said, setting down his Clarice Cliff teacup, "we've been telling stories a great deal longer than that. One to two million years ago, our transition from primates to humans began to engage language as a way of communicating with one another. Even before we spoke with words, human beings used their vocal chords to imitate birds or other animals."

When we try to imagine early humankind speaking, we begin with what they talked about. According to Professor Tobias, the "first primates had a hell of a lot to speak about." The parents had to teach their offspring how to survive, so the first communications were about practical things, functional things—for instance, teaching the young to make a certain kind of stone tool. Professor Tobias asked me to imagine him as one of our earliest ancestors, sharing information with his offspring:

> You see this tool. I use it for digging tubers and roots out of the ground. If you want to make a hand axe like this, you have to go out across the valley beyond the river and over to the next hill. At the very top of the hill, you will find a rock that has a fine grain and breaks predictably when hammered. It is a greenish rock. Try to break it. But make sure that you cut it along the grain; otherwise, it will shatter. Don't sit there too long because it will get dark and you will not be able to find your way back home.

We used stories to teach one another how to live. And where we shared these stories, community was formed. Storytelling is one means by which culture is recorded and transmitted because cultures depend on communication for transmission to take place between one generation and the next. Over millennia, this primitive form of storytelling evolved into a form of storytelling that is more inward looking and steeped with meaning.

The Brain's Hardwiring

It is often argued that storytelling is the most powerful and effective form of human communication because it is wired right into our brain hardware. Indeed, story is the brain's way of helping us make sense out of our lives, of creating coherence out of randomness and chaos. Most of our experience, our knowledge, and our thinking is organized as story.[2] It is our way of connecting with our own past (through memory), allowing us to make sense of what has happened to us, and planning for a future in which we envision certain outcomes taking place.

PET Scan Research

To substantiate theories that storytelling is a neurobiological function, scientists have made exciting discoveries about the capacities of our brain to tell and make sense of stories. Experiments have been conducted in which people have been placed in positron emission tomography (PET) scanners, which create images of brain activity in real time. Specific areas in the brain are found to light up when people are listening to various kinds of information. If someone is listening to just a grocery list, a particular part of the brain lights up. If the person is listening to a song, another part of the brain lights up. But if a person is listening to a story or telling a story, there are *a number* of specific areas of the brain that light up.[3]

Likewise, there is strong evidence that shows that patients with damage to certain parts of the brain are unable to tell stories or respond to them. This means that there are areas in the brain that are hardwired for the telling of and listening to stories.

What does brain hardwiring actually mean? It means that there is a network of brain cells that are involved with storytelling. When they fire, they wire together more tightly and efficiently. Telling stories is a way of strengthening those connections in the brain. The point is, storytelling is a skill that can be developed, a muscle that can be strengthened. We've certainly seen ample evidence of that through the work that we've been doing over the last two and a half decades. The more you tell stories, the better you get at it.

Principle 2. Everyone Has a Story

In all the years that I have done this work, I've never come across anyone who does not have a story. I've come across many who *believe* they don't. Whether you think your story is not important or urgent enough, or whether you think that other people in your company are the storytellers, I can tell you without hesitation that something has happened in your life that would make a great story. After completing our workshops, every participant— no matter their age or storytelling experience—emerges with a story that genuinely describes a life event. We simply have to know how to excavate for these events. This principle underlies much of Chapter 1. Knowing *why* we want to tell a story can be a catalyst for finding the story itself. For example, what's going on in our business or with our team right now that a story could address?

To get started, we recommend you locate a personal story to begin your training. A story that explains *how* you came to be where you are right now can be especially potent. We call this your "origin story." My origin story is the AIDS Day Program story, which you will read in all its detail in the first chapter. Then, having experienced the process of telling a story that's close to home for you, you will be prepared *to tell a business story in a personal way*. That means you will be comfortable with using all the emotional might and impact of a personal story toward a business aim.

Principle 3. Everyone Can Learn to Tell His or Her Story Better

We believe that your storytelling abilities will only improve with time and practice, but if you excavate and craft your story according to our What happened? method, to which we've dedicated Chapter 5, your storytelling can make a quantum leap forward. This method is deceptively simple. It states that interpretations, opinions, judgments, abstractions, concepts, and your thoughts and feelings about what happened are *not* story material. It's what your senses take in that is proven and effective content. If you answer the question "What happened?" according to these instructions, your story will unfold in a way that keeps listeners involved from start to finish.

With the What happened? method as a basis, there is no doubt that telling a story well is an art form with many parts to it. We need to conjure scenes and people, modulate our voices, move around the room, and keep connected to our listeners. By performing our own stories and teaching others to tell theirs, we have discovered a number of useful guidelines that are covered in Chapters 5, 6, and 7.

Principle 4. Everyone's Story Will Evolve

You may already be familiar with telling a story as part of your business communication, and you may think that the story you've been telling is the end-all story. You've told it once or twice to your team, and they all cheered at the end, so why not keep telling that winner?

We never discourage reusing a story with an established track record, but we do keep the door open to the likelihood that your story will evolve. It will evolve in the different listening environments where you present, allowing you to tailor your message as you speak, see how audiences react, and continue to develop nuance in the way you express your story. From the Narativ perspective, a good story evolves naturally, reflecting the reciprocal, mutually influential relationship of listening and telling. A good story is the spark of communication exchange.

Principle 5. Storytelling Is Every Person's Access to Creativity

The most basic definition of *creativity* is "the bringing together of already existing elements in a novel or surprising way." Creativity was long deemed the province of artists or those who had special talents and gifts, but we now recognize that creativity is also an essential part of what it is to be human.

Storytelling is the most democratic form of creativity because every human being has access to it. Your story is your birthright. In learning how to tell your story artfully by paying close attention to specific details, you are always creating something fresh and new. For example, many people have fallen in love, but no one has had *your* experience of falling in love. In telling your story, you have a tremendous opportunity to make creative choices. You can take a wide view of things, or you can zoom in, looking at particular details. You can make full use of each one of the senses in constructing your story.

The beauty of storytelling is that whether it is a business story or a personal one, the creativity and freedom of expression you bring to it are yours alone. In Chapter 4, we explore the creativity of storytelling through the Grandparent Exercise, a storytelling heuristic unique to the Narativ method.

Principle 6. There Is a Reciprocal Relationship Between Listening and Telling

We cannot tell a story if we don't feel that there is someone listening to us and paying attention. By the same token, we can't really listen to a story when the storyteller is not aware of his or her audience and is instead caught up in his or her own speech bubble. In this most basic sense, there is a reciprocal relationship between listening and telling. This principle lies at the very core of the Narativ method. It sounds simple. And it is. As you pay attention to it, you will discover more and more how it affects your communication. Our method provides a pathway to sensitize oneself to this dynamic relationship between listener and teller and to utilize it to tell effective stories. We'll look at this in depth in Chapter 2.

We often think that storytelling is mainly about presentation skills, but those skills are only one part of it. From our point of view, listening is of equal if not greater importance. Without it, storytelling simply isn't possible. So we always begin by looking at the *listening environment* in our work with businesses. You'll read how this principle has been applied at the companies we have profiled in this book and how you can apply this principle to your own communication needs.

I would like to highlight that ideal listening is based on nonjudgment. Nonjudgment in the Narativ method is considered a skill and a technique in and of itself, not an optional attitude toward our thoughts and feelings or those of others. That is because in terms of the purity of communication, judgment always muddies the waters.

EXCAVATING, CRAFTING, AND PRESENTING A STORY

The seven chapters of this book outline the steps of the Narativ method. Together, they form the process of excavating, crafting, and presenting your story. The diagram in Figure I.1 demonstrates the relationship of the chapters to the three parts of our method.

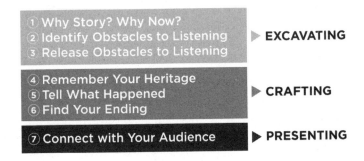

FIGURE I.1 **Excavating, Crafting, and Presenting**

Excavating

Excavation begins with the identification of your story. In which past event or series of events is your story located? Mine those events for the story itself. When excavating, we are like archeologists: we've found shards or half-buried jewels, but we need to dig the earth around those artifacts to see what else there is. Often, we'll find that our story is made up of more than the initial event that comes to mind—or even an entirely different memory or moment. To explore like this takes a certain mindset.

Storytelling involves both a critical mind and a creative mind. The critical mind analyzes, compares, and chooses, while the creative mind visualizes, foresees, and generates ideas. Since the critical mind tends to obstruct the creative mind, *the first principle of excavation is the deferment of judgment.* You must be allowed to express ideas without any concern for their value, feasibility, or significance. As you explore what material to use for your story, you allow yourself to become completely uncritical, making way for all sorts of ideas to come to mind. Only then do you bring back the power of critical thinking to become more rational and controlled as you craft and tell your story.

Crafting

When you're crafting your story, you'll begin to hone the ideas generated during the excavation phase, shaping them into a classic story structure of beginning, ending, and an emotional turning point in between. This phase is where the creativity of storytelling comes alive as you use the What happened? method to tell the story. You'll be surprised that in simply telling what happened, you'll discover so much choice. Each choice affects other choices, compelling and cajoling you to master the plot of your story.

While you're crafting, continue to keep an open mind to new ideas that may bubble up to the surface of your consciousness. It's natural to move back and forth a bit between excavation and crafting. A storyteller operates with some flexibility along with precision, and some patience along with enjoyment.

Presenting

Once you've excavated and crafted your story, you're ready to present. You'll speak without the need to refer to notes or PowerPoint slides. You'll know your ending, and you'll therefore have great confidence in where your story is going. No more guesswork and plenty of time to take your listeners on a journey. A key note here: When we talk about *a business story told in a personal way*, we're saying that your whole being is engaged in telling your story. You're bringing the vividness of the personal to the goals and aims of a business. When a story is told from that place of embodiment, it never fails to connect you with your audience. And that's your Lion's Gaze.

1

WHY STORY?
WHY NOW?

Why are you choosing to tell a *story* out of the many different ways human beings communicate? And why now? Why is this the moment to tell your story?

There is no right answer to these questions. They are meant to initiate an inquiry into your communication process. You might be telling a story to portray the best way to make a sales call, or to humanize a manager to a team that has faced crisis, or to depict pivotal moments that led to the formation of your enterprise so that new hires know who you are and why you exist as a company. Communication may have collapsed in a department, employees may be saying that they are unclear about the reasons for a merger or acquisition, or you may need to dramatize how policy changes in government will affect your client base. In answering these questions, you'll discover two consistent components: a rationale for storytelling and a call to action.

The Narativ approach to storytelling offers a step-by-step framework in which to excavate, craft, and present a story, beginning with this pair of questions. The more precisely and deeply you are able to answer them, the greater the focus of your storytelling effort will be.

I begin every corporate training with my origin story, my AIDS Day Program story, because it is a direct response to the questions Why story? Why now?

The story begins in 1990. I walked into a social services building on Willoughby Street in Brooklyn, down the stairs to the basement, looking for the "AIDS Day Program." On one of the doors was a white laboratory specimen box that said in red letters: "Danger. Hazardous Human Waste Material." I met with my supervisor, Dr. Mike Katch, who had a bushy gray moustache and one blue and one green eye. He told me that I was to give the clients what they needed, psychologically and emotionally. I shared an office with other social work interns. There were blue vinyl floors, and fluorescent lights buzzed overhead. There were no windows. Paintings made by the patients adorned the walls.

Ronald, my first client, sat across my desk.

"How are you?" I asked.

"I'm dying," he said.

"What do you need?" I asked.

He told me he wanted to marry his girlfriend, Yvonne.

I told Dr. Katch that Ronald was delusional as a result of suffering from lethal cryptococcal meningitis. As a clinical psychologist, I was trained to work with patients who would gain insight and grow from reflecting on their experiences. "He's got no insight," I said.

"It's not about insight," Katch replied. "It's about being alive in this moment. If Ronald and Yvonne want to get married, that's their choice. In social work we start with the client, not with fancy psychobabble. There's no time to reflect. Their story is happening now, in this moment."

Some weeks later I looked down into Ronald's open casket. He was dressed in a gray suit, a white shirt, and a red tie with a yellow rose in his lapel. Yvonne came up to me. "I just got married, and I'm already a widow. At least he died knowing he was loved." Ronald's name was engraved on a brass plate that read: "In Memoriam." The plate was the size of a packet of chewing gum, and it was hammered onto a wooden board with at least 50 other names at the entrance to the AIDS Day Program building.

I sobbed in Katch's office. He gave me a tissue. "At least Ronald had Yvonne. Most of these patients are dying, leaving nothing behind. Nothing. Everything they own ends up in black garbage bags. And no one ever comes to claim their belongings." Their stories were all they had, and they were dying without having told them. I told Katch that I wanted to start a storytelling circle so that the clients could leave their stories behind to be retold and passed on by others. And those who live can carry others' stories into the future.

I went into the dayroom where all the patients congregated and said, "I'm starting a storytelling group."

"What the f--cking hell, Murray, what are they teaching you in that social work school? What are you talking about? I don't have a story. I'm a crack addict," Sharon responded. "Do you understand? This is how I got infected." She had no teeth. She wore gold rings on every single one of her fingers. She said, "I've spent my whole life in the alleys of Brooklyn scoring crack."

I said, "Yes, that's your story. That's what I want to hear. Just tell me what happened to you. That's what I want to know. What happened to you?"

By Christmas 1994, my storytelling group was filled with people. One of the clients, Harriet, said to me, "My daughter, who is three, will never really know who I was because I'm going to die before she can hear my story. Would you mind if we made a videotape of my story? So that I can leave her that videotape as a legacy of who I am after I die?" We did. After that, all the clients in my program wanted legacy tapes.

Newspapers published articles every single week on the number of people infected with and dying of AIDS. By 1995, the *New York Times* reported 159,000 people had died.

At that time, the Department of AIDS Services of New York announced cutbacks, and this affected people in my program. Everyone gathered in wheelchairs or bent over canes, they got on a bus, and they went up to the state capitol in Albany. They left videotapes of their legacy stories on the desks of the legislators, accompanied by a handwritten note:

> Listen to these stories. Listen to my story. Listen to what happened to me, and then tell me that I don't deserve services. As the numbers you read every day in the papers continue escalating, they become increasingly meaningless. Those in power who are supposed to be affected by these numbers are in fact not responding. The mayor of New York is denying what's going on. The president is denying it. Organizations aren't responding fast enough. Pharmaceutical companies aren't doing research fast enough or presenting medications fast enough. But we are not numbers. This is our lives!

The legislators listened to their pleas for civil rights and funding for AIDS research. Laws were enacted that prohibited discrimination against people with HIV/AIDS in all workplace settings, state and municipal services, public accommodations, commercial facilities, transportation, and telecommunications. *This happened because people told their stories.*

My experience during this unprecedented epidemic inspired me to distill all I knew about listening and storytelling into the Narativ method. I understood that at a particular moment in time, there is always a reason to use a story rather than graphs, statistical charts, Power-Points, and all the other forms of communication. Stories are powerful. They change lives. I tell the AIDS Day Program story because it exemplifies the emotional impact of story, the social and cultural role of story, and its practical efficacy in creating change. It is also my origin story; it shows how storytelling became the focus of my 30-plus-year career.

Drawing on that experience, I developed the prompt Why story? Why now? to use at the start of every storytelling engagement. It pulls us out of vagueness into specificity; it helps us identify and pursue our storytelling objective. Let's look at an example.

Craig Kostelic, the chief business officer of Condé Nast's Food Innovation Group (FIG), views every member of his team as a storyteller. He told us, "It's the common trait that links every job. Whether you're in editing, telling stories to consumers, or you're in sales, telling a story to a client or marketing team or closing deals or getting authorizations, or you're in creative services, telling stories to bring numbers to life, we are *all* storytellers." For Craig, storytelling is "the most important and transferable skill set that we all have as part of our professional development."

As we spoke with Craig, he shared an unequivocal understanding that storytelling joins the head to the heart—it brings to life with emotional power the data, facts, and figures embedded in concepts such as cost-benefit analysis and return on investment (ROI). These stories engage and connect. Connection builds audiences and gets them on board. Why story? was abundantly evident for Craig.

But Why now? Why engage Narativ to help FIG tell better stories right now?

In an explosive period of growth in Condé Nast's recent history, the Food Innovation Group was blazing a path ahead in digital storytelling, and FIG had become somewhat renowned inside the company. Craig sought out Narativ for a keynote speech to help take FIG's storytelling to the next level. He also saw story as a way to communicate the power of belonging and teamwork within FIG. He felt that belonging and teamwork had been essential to their success, so it was a message he wanted to reinforce and celebrate.

Every company that approaches Narativ has a different response to Why story? Why now? Storytelling and stories are two sides of the most important competency in business communication. Storytelling puts all of us in the position to know our work more deeply and intimately through a story. Meanwhile, stories themselves work all kinds of magic on communication, from delivering emotional relevance to bringing data to life to transferring knowledge in an engaging and memorable way. In the following chapters, you'll read about how companies have successfully applied the Narativ method to achieve their business communication goals. Here are some examples that will be explained in detail:

- A social media company's marketing teams were promoting its business globally, but within the company the marketing teams were not always seen as being as essential as the engineers. As a result, they wanted to communicate their stake in the business and show their value in an impactful way. That was their answer to Why story? Why now? Then came a second answer: "We need to be better listeners." We designed training that was entirely about identifying and releasing obstacles to listening so that everyone in the entire department could be better listeners within their various teams and to their business partners, which paved the way for powerful stories to emerge. You'll read more about what happened in Chapter 2.

- A tech company was pivoting, which required reorganization and rethinking, and this made waves in its management culture. We were asked to create a listening and storytelling environment in which to identify and release obstacles that were preventing clear and clean communication, and then develop a new, forward-thinking story to help them move ahead. Chapter 3 goes into depth about the application of our method for navigating crisis.

- A media and entertainment giant was bringing together 140 employees from 47 emerging market countries for a corporate retreat. The manager wanted an event that would "break down boundaries among people." The manager told us that the event had to be "really good because some participants were from countries whose governments hated one another." Their Why story? Why now? revealed an intense need for collaboration and connection in order to tackle the enormity of their assignment. Read about it in Chapter 4.

- A national medical insurance company was trying to change the perception that the company was a large behemoth out of touch with the customers' real needs. For this company's leaders, the questions Why story? Why now? revealed that it was in fact a customer-centric company that wasn't putting a spotlight on how its customer service department responded to real client needs. Over the years, the company had invested significantly in training to go beyond the call of duty and exceed expectations. The question made us turn to the managers and employees in the call centers that addressed clients directly. This led to excavating stories of actual customer experiences that brought to life how the company was making a difference in the lives of its customers, challenging the narrative that had been in the media until then. You'll read their story in Chapter 5.

- A multinational pharmaceutical firm's sales and research teams frequently made dry, fact-filled presentations that were so data heavy that it was hard to read what was on each slide of the decks. Some decks were 80 slides long! Their Why story? Why now? was at first related to standard presentation concerns: they wanted to tell stories that engaged, and they adapted presentation decks to those personal stories. And then, as often happens in the process of answering these questions, a second reason arose, even more powerful than the first. The research and sales teams had different agendas and purposes, yet they had to find a common language so that the whole enterprise could move forward. "What stories can we tell that would help us be better collaborators and therefore create better presentations?" they asked. Find this also in Chapter 5.

- The chief business officer of an iconic publishing brand sought to craft a story to rouse his team and form stronger bonds. I worked closely with him to create his story, and in Chapter 6 you'll observe the real-world process of excavating, crafting, and preparing for presentation in minute detail.

- A luxury brand's legal team was often seen as creating headaches for the multitude of businesses the company held, and the team members needed to position the team as a business partner to the rest of the company. The team's answer to Why story? Why now? was to change that perception by telling powerful stories that would touch people's hearts and get past preconceptions. You'll read their story and its surprising twist in Chapter 7.

There are common themes and purposes that emerge from asking the questions Why story? Why now? Here are some of them. Feel free to add your own:

- Demonstrate leadership

- Explain a raison d'être and purpose

- Increase collaboration or teamwork

- Generate empathy

- Inspire change

- Resolve conflict

- Humanize or dimensionalize an issue or audience

- Share learning or training

- Celebrate and build culture

Now, take a moment to reflect on a project or initiative at work, some relational issues within a team, or a newly identified target audience. Why would you use story to support that work? And what about this moment in time requires the story to be told? Explore the center and edges of those questions. You will gain greater insight the deeper you probe.

As we move forward from this starting point, excavation evolves into a process of exploration and discovery.

Roll up your sleeves because stories require some digging. They are not ready-made, a product you pull off the shelf. In fact, viewing them that way diminishes their return. A good example is formulaic training material or a clichéd inspirational phrase. They lack the direction and urgency of Why story? Why now? and the vitality of a good story. Work needs to be done to get to the heart of the matter. There've been no surprises yet. We haven't pushed through any boundaries. And this is precisely why we must suspend judgment for a period of time: so that we don't cut short the creative process of excavation and miss out on stories that lie just below the surface. The obstacles that stand in the way, which we explore in the next two chapters, turn out to be part of the creative process itself.

IDENTIFY OBSTACLES TO LISTENING

The best way to deliver information is by first understanding your listening environment and then telling a story.

—Russ Charlton,
former vice president of internal auditing at Time Warner

If we were in a Narativ training together right now, your listening would be creating my speaking, and my speaking would be creating your listening. We would have already entered into a feedback loop with one another even though we barely knew each other. Telling shapes listening. Listening shapes telling. The feedback loop we are describing is, according to the Narativ method, precisely what transformed communication actually looks like: it's when you pay heed to the reciprocal relationship between listening and telling.

When we say there is a reciprocal relationship between listening and telling, we mean that they are mutually influential. Speaking and listening influence each other throughout any conversation or presentation. Any shift in one creates a shift in the other. As we seek to connect with our audience—and to maintain that connection—being sensitive to this natural dynamic is essential (see Figure 2.1).

FIGURE 2.1 **Reciprocal Relationship Between Listening and Telling**

What impedes this flow are what we call in Narativ parlance "obstacles to listening." As noted earlier, we prioritize listening in our method. Therefore, for successful communication to take place in the time and space we've allocated for it, we should identify and release any obstacles to listening so that they don't affect the telling.

Russ Charlton, the former VP of internal auditing at Time Warner, who brought in Narativ to Time Warner to address the blockages to listening and telling, told us about his experience of the importance of listening:

I remember your saying to be aware of what's going on around you. That really stuck with me. Just sitting here now, there are people having normal conversations over breakfast, noises from the kitchen, the clanking of plates. Every time a car goes by, there's a distracting reflection on the wall behind me. I have to be aware of the listening environment to know whether you and I are making a connection and adjust to that.

Do I need to raise or lower my voice? Should I lean in closer? All those things were a vital part of training our auditors on how to be better listeners and better communicators. If I want to engage deeply with a human resources manager or an employee who has a personal matter, I turn over my phone and push it away so that I can fully engage with the individual. Then the first thing you do is close your mouth and listen to what people are telling you because you are going to interview people about their area of expertise. I'm not a cloud computer expert or a data privacy expert, and neither are the people on my team, but the people we are interviewing should be, and so we go in and listen to them. To be able to tell an effective story, first you have to be able to listen.

Listening may be likened to a container, and story may be likened to the liquid that is poured into the container. The container gives shape to the liquid in the same way that the listening gives shape to the story (see Figure 2.2). This may seem obvious, but it is experientially profound. Pay attention to it in your next conversation.

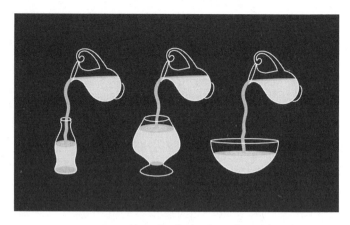

FIGURE 2.2 **Listening Is the Container that
Gives Shape to the Telling**

This recognition of the reciprocal relationship between listening and telling becomes a lens through which
to examine the communication environment in any organization. When Narativ goes into companies to address
communication issues, we first look for what gets in the
way of that dynamic. What gets in the way of listening?
What's shaping the telling? If, for example, team members prioritize competition over collaboration, as we
discovered they were at a large social media company,
then competition is setting the tone of the communication. What is it like to tell stories in a competitive environment? What happens to your listening? At Narativ
we consider this first stage of our communication assess-
ment as ethnographic: we are looking at the culture of an
organization or department broadly to determine trends
in communication obstacles.

Let's explore how first we identify obstacles to listening and then how we release those obstacles in a real-world example. The end goal is always clear communication. With clear communication, any objective can be achieved.

IDENTIFYING THE OBSTACLES TO LISTENING

Narativ was invited to present our listening and storytelling method to 14 global marketing teams at a social media company. The leaders of the marketing group wanted us to focus entirely on listening because they felt that storytelling was already so much a part of the company's DNA. Although this example appears to address only listening, you will quickly see how listening and telling never live apart. We heard from managers at this company, "Everyone's talking, everyone's telling stories, but our teams are not listening to each other. How do we help them listen and therefore collaborate better?" I appreciated their conundrum and the way they approached it. In our work with technology companies in the midst of rapid growth, I've often observed a recognition of the importance of empathy in interpersonal relationships as a means to evolve communication. This, of course, has everything to do with listening and telling.

People who work at large technology companies are often single-minded, ambitious, and competitive. Although these qualities are syntonic with the company's driven corporate culture, they do not align with the aspiration for staff to support one another's successes and thereby foster stronger bonds within the team. In fact, there's a tendency to blame others when things go wrong, which leads to conflict, resentment, and breakdowns in mutual understanding. Employees talk over one another or attempt to dominate in conversations and meetings. The core problem is that people lose touch with the fact that collaboration and communication depend on listening.

Employee engagement surveys conducted before we visited verified that communication and transparency are the two most challenging areas in the culture of this social media company. Whereas a fast-paced, multitasking approach is often seen as a virtue at technology companies, the marketing leaders had identified a need to develop mutual *understanding* and *empathy* in the communication styles of their teams. The challenge was to transform current conversation modalities so that members of the 14 marketing teams, each dealing with a different audience, would be motivated to support one another toward the achievement of shared performance goals. This included identifying and addressing personal and cultural obstacles to listening and building a skill set to move members away from disconnection toward empathy. We provided a hands-on, experiential approach to identifying obstacles to listening at the company's campus in California.

Let me drop you into the training to demonstrate how obstacles to listening may be identified in the moment-to-moment of communication. As I always do, I began with my AIDS Program story followed by a brief Listening Contemplation exercise. This contemplation asked people to become aware of their immediate surroundings and then progressively to move to introspection, simply noticing when obstacles emerged throughout. Let's start with that contemplation, which is usually done with eyes closed.

Listening Contemplation Exercise

Take a moment now, sitting at your desk or at home, to follow the steps of the contemplation. When it speaks about the "group," feel free to tune in to who is around you in your office, to visualize your team, or simply continue being aware of your environment:

1. Bring your attention to any sounds that there may be in this room. And without calling anything out or saying anything out aloud, just acknowledge to yourself what you hear when you tune in to this room.

2. Now bring your awareness to outside of this room. What do you hear outside of this room? Anything? Are you aware of any sound outside of this room? Come back into the room again. Pay attention. Listen. What are you aware of? What's happening in your mind?

3. Now bring your attention to this group of people whom you're sitting among at the moment. What do you hear from the group of people seated? Bring your attention to the space between you and your neighbor or neighbors if you've got one person on either side, one person behind you, and one person in front of you. What do you hear?

4. Now bring your awareness into your own body, back into your body. Listen with your brain. Now shift your listening, and listen from your heart. What changes when you listen from your heart? Bring your awareness down to your gut. Start to listen with your gut. What do you notice? And finally, with your feet, listen with your feet. Take a few breaths to relax.

What obstacles arose for you as you read? Note them. Later in the chapter we will provide some tools for categorizing these obstacles. Obstacles can be very light—for example, birds chirping outside the room. We might not even normally call this an obstacle. Birdsong can be quite pleasing and enjoyable. Nevertheless, those sounds are in our listening, part of our listening environment, so we note them.

Now think about your office: what listening obstacles are there in your work environment? Take a moment to list these obstacles and see how they differ or connect with the obstacles you've already noted. What is it like to become aware of them from a nonjudgmental perspective? Just simply noting them prepares you for moving past them.

After guiding the audience through this contemplation, I reached out for feedback. If you want to know what obstacles to listening are in your audience, the best way to find out is to ask them:

"I was trying very hard not to think about my phone in my pocket."

"I became irritated when I heard paper crinkling."

"I couldn't get my to-do list out of my head."

"I hear my baby crying even though I'm across the country."

"I felt super connected to you while recalling my own memories of people from that time."

"I kept going back to past experiences habitually each morning, so I was replaying those in my mind and then losing my focus."

"I felt a lot of irritation in my body as I slowed down and tried to pay attention to the exercise."

These responses are revealing of common obstacles people encounter in the work environment. Other obstacles can be more subtle and difficult to identify.

Alex, a participant in the training, shared that he was having a hard time listening because my presentation seemed a little "goofy." I wasn't sure what he meant by that, so I asked him to explain.

"Like, I can't take you seriously. This cynical side of me takes over. I wonder if I'm just being manipulated. I've got opinions on how presentations should be, and I'm judging you."

The ability to truly hear others' obstacles requires listening without judgment, opinion, and rationalization. Rather than penetrating Alex's judgment, arguing with him or being defensive, which would most likely throw fuel onto the fire and make his opinions even stronger, instead, I thanked Alex for his honesty, and I let him know that I had heard what he'd said: that he'd judged me and had thought, "I can't listen to this guy because what he's saying sounds goofy and manipulative."

Imagine if I had taken Alex's comment personally and had felt insulted or humiliated. I could have retorted that there is a thorough scientific basis to my methods and that they'd worked successfully with thousands of others in the technology field. That would have been just me defending myself—and not listening to him.

I would like to make special note here that the statement "I hear you" has been co-opted into corporate parlance to a certain degree as a way of shutting people up. In our method, if you don't mean it, don't say it. In that way, the listening of both parties is genuine and flows freely.

Alex responded, "What would you suggest I do to circumvent that sort of continued cynicism because it shows up in my work all the time? How do I get to a place of positivity, of being open, when things are not necessarily what I would initially connect to?"

Here's the opening for Alex to notice his tendency to make judgments and close down. In the Narativ method we're acutely aware that trying to push these thoughts away is like feeding them Miracle-Gro. They'll just get stronger. In other words, don't judge your own judgment. Just be aware of it and observe it.

I suggested Alex try a different tack and simply note, "There goes my mind again, doing that same old judging thing." To take it a little further, I suggested he ask himself, "What am I gaining by having that kind of judgment? What am I losing by having that kind of judgment?" What he gains is a sense of superiority and separateness. He holds himself apart. What he loses is a sense of connection with himself and with others. He loses the opportunity of understanding.

By simply asking what the obstacles were, we unveiled the power that judgment has to interfere. We added it to our growing list on the room's whiteboard. "Sounds, to-do lists, body irritation, *judgment*." Next, let's look at technology itself as an obstacle to listening.

TECHNOLOGY: A DEEP DIVE

"Even though I had it on silent, it was buzzing and vibrating."

At the most obvious level, Kareem's phone is an external obstacle—that is, an outside force that affects his listening. However, it also operates on a physical level, vibrating against his thigh. Many recent studies also show how device sounds and alarms produce a stress reaction in the body.[1]

Kareem tells us that he's trying hard not to think about his phone. Not only is this *thought* an additional obstacle to listening but so is the feeling or emotion associated with the thought. I ask him about that. He says, "It's all about the to-do list, being in control. I'm constantly worried about all this stuff that needs to get done, running out of time, not getting to deadlines, and disappointing people."

When I push him to go deeper, Kareem tells me that his concern is ultimately about self-preservation and survival and that if he's really honest with himself, he's in a constant state of fear.

Kareem is not alone. So much of what drives obstacles to listening is fear on a primitive and visceral level—that worry, that anxiety, that sense of "what's going to happen if I ignore my phone?" It serves us tremendously well to be able to identify the obstacle of fear in our own listening because so many times our knee-jerk reactions to things are based on unacknowledged fear. Instead of recognizing the fear in ourselves, we project it onto someone or something else.

"So you worry about being in trouble then?" I ask Kareem. "Is there a power dimension as well?"

He responds, "Ultimately, yes, the fear is 'you'll be in trouble,' that someone's going to see what you've done, and there'll be repercussions."

I thank him for his honesty and for revealing this insecurity. His statement corroborates our own findings that a tremendous obstacle to listening is *relational* power dynamics.

This simple group exercise revealed all kinds of obstacles to listening. They had mainly to do with the mind's constant chatter or physical discomforts. But there are *psychological* (emotional) obstacles to listening too, such as longing, memories, and loss. And as we saw with Kareem, there are relational obstacles to listening, such as power: Who is speaking, and are we listening to them from a place of powerlessness or fear? Has something transpired in the past that fills our listening with criticism or judgment? We may feel justified in our stance based on past experiences or other habitual emotions (for example, "I'm someone who's just uncomfortable in meetings"), but these create a stumbling block to our productivity. Even obstacles that are not personal, that are part of a corporate culture, can be noticed and related to.

In Table 2.1, let's look at the array of obstacles to listening the teams identified during breakout groups and how they sought to address them.

Open listening takes a leap of trust. Through their willingness to listen to one another, team members demonstrated that they were able to place principles ahead of personalities and to suspend emotional reactivity in the service of the well-being of the team and its goals.

However many obstacles reveal themselves in a listening contemplation or group check-in, in our method

TABLE 2.1	Case Study: Global Marketing Teams' Listening Session	
Categories of Obstacles to Listening	**Obstacles Uncovered**	**Addressing the Obstacles**
External	Distance between teams Multiple conversations Organization size Room noise, pings, chatter, beeps Signals getting lost in the noise—lots of channels, hard to sort Time Devices Other distractions (people walking by, deliveries, and so on) Floor culture Culture of speed plus distractions Multitasking Urgent versus important	Maintain a safe environment in which to bring up issues without a solution. Manage time. Maintain rules of engagement for meetings. Create time and space for collaboration. Listen without laptops and mobile phones. Use tools to help navigate the noise. Use more in-person time (or video conferences). Run better meetings.
Physical	Lack of sleep Hunger Hot or cold Antsy, overexcited	Meditation: If it works for you, Do it! Eat. Add and/or remove layers. Walk outside.

Categories of Obstacles to Listening	Obstacles Uncovered	Addressing the Obstacles
Internal	Pressure to say something Lack of time No patience Lack of focus Assuming negative intent Interruptions and/or people talking over one another Pressure to capture everything Thinking while listening Imposter syndrome—wanting to be the expert Always in the future instead of in the moment Hesitating to speak	Be aware of collaboration. Focus on strengths and differences. Decline meetings when not needed. Be honest with yourself, manager, and team about what you can contribute. Do research before meetings. We make hybrid ideas and output including desired outcomes. Don't assume positive or negative intent.
Psychological	Lack of empathy Ego Decision already made and/or multiple agendas Judging work before listening No personal time Fear of not belonging	Have fun. Come into conversations with an open mind. Meditation: If it works for you, Do it!
Relational	Don't know each other; don't know personal lives and roles	Define the roles of communication channels. Share common goals.

Categories of Obstacles to Listening	Obstacles Uncovered	Addressing the Obstacles
	Conflicts	Share your truth.
	Want to please	Share your story.
	Lack of trust	Demand feedback.
	Lack of inclusion or perspectives	Love each other.
		No one is a vacuum.
	Not understanding other person	Allow the quiet voices to speak and be heard.
	No rules	Approach meetings with respect.
	Not being in the moment	
	Lack of alignment	Maintain transparency and state common goals.
	Overall lack of commitment	Share goals and vision among team members.
	Won't speak up	Set expectations. Communicate what's important to you with your team and partners.
	Solutions proposed without understanding the problem	
	Goal misalignment	Create a common language.
	No context	
	No shared goals	Create a priority toolbox.
	Vague authority structure (no clear system of accountability)	Ownership: We own this.
	Lead versus support	
	Cultural and/or global differences	
	No follow-through	
	Language: Different experiences and/or perspectives	*(continued)*

Categories of Obstacles to Listening	Obstacles Uncovered	Addressing the Obstacles
Relational (continued)	Different terms and competing priorities	
	Weight: Whom to listen to?	
	Ownership	
	Saying no without consideration	
	Lack of face-to-face contact	
	Lack of common language	
	Diverse backgrounds	
	Madison Avenue versus Silicon Valley—clashing cultures	

we take the position that there is nothing wrong with the obstacles to listening. They just are. We notice them. In fact, just to notice them sometimes takes real self-awareness. Simple-seeming obstacles can be tied to deeper fears and undercurrents that run within a company. These are things that have become embedded in an organization's culture, and they *should* be identified and acknowledged. The number of obstacles to listening of which we're not usually aware is surprising. Open listening challenges our habits of ignoring. It requires a commitment to go beyond all those obstacles, to keep them out of the listening space. Finally, identifying the obstacles helps us give the gift of listening.

The Narativ method, unlike many storytelling techniques, seeks to understand a business's specific culture or a team's working atmosphere, "the listening environment," as the platform for change. As an individual in a company's culture, your listening is the lightning rod for those obstacles, allowing you to identify and then release them, as we will discuss in the next chapter.

CATEGORIES OF OBSTACLES TO LISTENING

As a guideline to approach the listening environment in your organization, we've provided the following five categories. They form the core of our ethnographic approach, and you'll be reading more about them as the book progresses. Narativ's cofounder, Paul Browde, MD, helped develop this list in the early days of our method.

We have made an exhaustive categorization of obstacles to listening because it's the awareness of them that gets the process of releasing them started. So much is swept under the rug in ordinary communication. To be resilient, present communicators, alive to the reciprocal relationship between listening and telling, we need to clearly understand all types of obstacles that present themselves. This kind of expertise is a communication skill we benefit from developing.

External Obstacles

Hearing is the physical perception of sound, in which sound waves are received by the eardrum and then, through a complex set of mechanical interactions involving very small bones, are translated into nerve impulses that travel to the brain, where they are interpreted into meaning. Hearing is one component of listening. As the sound and tone of the words enter the body, they cause a wide range of effects. The quality of the sound of a voice can cause feelings in the body. Some voices are musical and sooth-ing, whereas others are harsh and unsettling. Notice how the sound of a voice can alter your breathing. Some voices cause you to take deep, slow breaths, resulting in a wave of relaxation through your body. Other voices cause you to take short, sharp breaths, resulting in a level of anxiety and perhaps irritation.

Other hearing obstacles to listening include the most obvious ones—noises and other sounds, such as traffic, barking dogs, jackhammers, music, or whirring air con-ditioners. This also includes an excessively loud voice. How can you possibly listen to what someone is saying if he or she is trying to command your attention by yelling or shouting? All you can hear is the shouting.

Seeing is the physical perception of visual stimulus through the eyes, in which images are perceived and communicated to the brain for interpretation. How does what you are seeing affect your ability to listen? If the storyteller looks sad, does that increase the level of attention you bring to his or her speaking? Does it decrease it? If somebody looks disheveled and unkempt, are you likely to listen with the same degree of attention as you would if that person were neatly dressed in an expensive suit? What judgments arise from seeing?

Smelling is the physical perception of olfactory stimulus through the nose and into the brain. How does the smell in the room affect your ability to listen? Does a strong perfume or scented candle interfere with your concentration? Does the smell of a crackling fire in the hearth induce a feeling of coziness and comfort, allowing greater listening?

Physical Obstacles

These most often have to do with the body's physical needs: hunger, needing to go to the bathroom, tiredness, physical discomfort or pain, sexual arousal, clothing that's too tight or uncomfortable, rashes, feeling sick, or even having a bad hair day!

Internal Obstacles

Internal obstacles include thoughts, memories, emotions, and feelings. You can have a variety of feelings in an hour, even within a minute, especially if you are upset or sad, or feel extreme happiness or joy. These can be obstacles to listening. Some of these obstacles are invisible to others and often to ourselves.

We use the general term *noise* to refer to the constant chatter that is going on in our minds. This noise consists mostly of free-floating thoughts that vary in intensity and may include shopping lists, ruminating over a recent argument, or obsessive preoccupations. "Did I turn off the stove?" "Did I pay the phone bill?" "I wish I could get that song out of my head!"

Psychological Obstacles

Judgments of others and ourselves make it difficult to listen and be creative. "I am not good enough." "He is better than I am." "She doesn't know how to tell a story." Opinions or strong beliefs of agreement or disagreement can interfere if the listener likes or dislikes what the storyteller is saying. Opinions about religion, politics, or other topics may be obstacles to listening.

Interpretations refers to the meanings we create about others or ourselves. "I am a failure" is an example of meaning attributed to a particular set of life circumstances. It is difficult to tell an empowering story with this interpretation.

Similarly, when a listener interprets the life of the storyteller, it limits the ability of the latter to create freely. If we think, "This manager is a disaster, and he is clearly still under the influence of the person he replaced," we inadvertently may be creating that story in the teller. Even if you think the interpretation is kind, it interferes with listening. Avoid bringing your own analysis or caretaking to someone else's story. Judgments of others and ourselves make it difficult to be generative and creative.

Relational Obstacles

The relationships we have with people often shape the way we listen to them. Usually, one person is in a more powerful position than the other. The way you listen to your parents or siblings is different from the way you listen to a police officer who pulls you over for speeding or your doctor who calls you in to discuss the results of a test. We've all seen how a son listens to his father giving advice after a soccer game or a young girl looks up to her grandmother. Imagine different people telling you the same information—see how each relationship influences how you hear what's being said. At work, there is a hierarchy, and that's a natural and important structure.

Bringing awareness to how the hierarchy affects our listening is crucial so that we don't let it influence open listening. This is not to dismiss or undermine necessary power structures but simply to be aware of how our ideas about them affect what we hear. Otherwise, we may not contribute all that we can, or conversely, we may not allow our leaders or subordinates to contribute their best.

•   •   •

Understanding what blocks us from listening to ourselves and to others is fundamental to the Narativ method. You will not receive the benefits of the method unless you fully understand and implement the basic concept that there is a reciprocal relationship between listening and storytelling. My listening must be clear for me to be present with you, and your listening must be clear for you to be present with me. We have a lot of power as listeners. Use it well!

Once we've identified these obstacles, we intend to let them go. That is essential to our method. When we want to listen, it is not the time to address or hold on to any obstacles. It is the time to release them in favor of listening and participating. We can always get back to our to-do list or take up more challenging interpersonal conversations later. We can incorporate what comes to us into an inventory of observations to use to address larger issues. But when it comes to listening and storytelling—

the immediate act of communication we seek to accomplish through our method—we let go of obstacles to listening. This, like everything in our method, takes practice. We're unlearning old habits and activating potential. To listen without judgment in particular is surprisingly difficult, but the more you do it, the more you—and your team—will reap the rewards.

BEING YOUR OWN
BEST LISTENER

At Narativ, we always say, "Listening begins with you." This may seem ironic after we've put so much emphasis on the reciprocal relationship of listening and telling. But in a sense, it is the most powerful key to successful communication, collaboration, and giving mutual support. Learning how to listen to ourselves first will heighten our ability to listen to others (Figure 2.3).

Listening to oneself is a form of introspection. We each have the ability to be reflective of our own story by asking, "What are the obstacles in my listening to the story I'm telling?" For example, if I am to address a sales team, as I imagine them as my audience, what obstacles arise for me? Fear. Discomfort. Is there someone I am attracted to, or do I harbor some resentment toward a coworker? This is all natural, normal, and human, and we make no

FIGURE 2.3 **Listening Begins with You**

claim to solve these obstacles with the method. But we recognize that they get in the way of our listening and our performance. So we identify them and let them be rather than suppress them or use other common psychological tactics. In a sense, being aware of them enhances our storytelling because there's nothing under the rug, nothing hidden holding us back. It takes a little courage to bring forth these obstacles, but that courage creates an open field for our storytelling.

This type of introspection is not about being preoccupied with ourselves. Even when we are alone, it posits an audience in our listening, and therefore we're always in a reciprocal mode. It can be enormously helpful to analyze how one is approaching a team by identifying the audience, then the obstacles, and finally, releasing them so you can proceed. Releasing the obstacles is the counterpart to identifying them, and it is the topic of our next chapter.

LISTENING IS THE BEGINNING

Listening is the beginning of the transformation of communication in business. How often do we hear, "They were not listening to me"? How often do we feel the presence of distraction in our exchanges with others? And how much do these experiences reflect deeper trends within our company's culture that play a role in decreasing productivity and job satisfaction?

We might say that we can change this by simply paying adequate attention, but we need a more compelling understanding of how communication takes place. The reciprocal relationship of listening and telling provides that framework. Within its boundaries, we can use our ears, our entire bodies, and our brain's incredible abilities to take in information openly and without judgment, knowing that listener and teller play equal roles in the success of the exchange.

So begin paying attention to how *you* listen and how that affects the telling of your team members. Just as listening starts with you, so does change, and we can all be change agents in our organization when we listen.

LISTENING AND EXCAVATING

When you practice identifying obstacles to listening, you will notice that many of your obstacles have to do with past experiences and memories. One of the reasons we do not suppress the obstacles but just make note of them and let them be is that some of them can be material for our stories. Therefore, identifying obstacles to listening not only paves the way to releasing obstacles but also can potentially lead to identifying an experience or memory that could become a story. So pay attention to your obstacles because your next great story might be hiding in plain sight.

Now, take a moment to listen to yourself and identify your obstacles to listening at this very moment. Use Table 2.2 to categorize your obstacles.

TABLE 2.2 Listening to Yourself and Identifying Your Obstacles to Listening		
Categories of Obstacles to Listening	**Examples**	**My Obstacles Are . . .**
External	Air-conditioning	
	E-mail pinging	
	Horn honking	
	Birds chirping	
	Whirring of technology devices	
Physical	Hunger	
	Thirst	
	Need to go to the bathroom	
	Pain (back, stomach, or something else)	
	Adrenaline rush	
Internal	Thoughts (to-do list, questions that pop up randomly)	
	Memories (for example, my football days)	
	Emotions and feelings (anger, fear, sadness, excitement)	
Psychological	Interpretations: "I am a failure." "They're successful."	*(continued)*

Categories of Obstacles to Listening	Examples	My Obstacles Are ...
Psychological (continued)	Judgments: "I don't think I'm the person for the job." "She's way better than I am." Opinions: "I believe that all religious expressions need to be banned in the office."	
Relational	Hierarchical: Who works for you? Whom do you work for? What obstacles get in the way of your ability to collaborate more productively?	

RELEASE
OBSTACLES
TO LISTENING

n our Monday morning meetings at Narativ, we put releasing obstacles to listening at the top of the agenda.

"I'm leaving for California this afternoon, and I have still a number of items to prepare for my presentation, in addition to booking a car. I'm a little scattered. Plus, it's hot out, and I'm aware of what moving through that heat will be like." Katy pauses. "That's it. That's what's in my listening." The rest of the Narativ team acknowledges her comments with a "thank you." Then the next person speaks. "I'm preoccupied by the number of tasks I have today: checking off remaining items on the marketing checklist, social media posting, and some calls. I'm juggling all of those and working through how best to prioritize," says Michael.

That is releasing the obstacles to listening. For the speaker, identifying and releasing are closely related. You take a moment to scan for what obstacles there are from the categories in Chapter 2. By speaking them to the group, you release them. Listeners are asked to suspend judgment. We remove the usual chatter of opinion and commentary that runs in our minds when someone is speaking.

Releasing the obstacles lets your colleagues know that if you seem distracted or annoyed, for example, it's because of your own preoccupations that have nothing to do with them. This is important if you're in a leadership role because people are watching your responses and often taking them personally. With this practice, you enhance focus on the meeting at hand, enabling a purer strain of attention than one fettered by miscellaneous concerns and issues.

Releasing the obstacles to listening may be used as a general communication protocol before any meeting or conversation, because it provides a quick way to open up communication and create connection, which in turn heightens attention to the matters at hand. However, it is important to understand the roots of this practice. It derives from a component of our methodology that we call preparing a "dedicated time and space" for listening and storytelling.

A DEDICATED TIME AND SPACE

A key element in storytelling is the performance environment. A useful example is a night at the theater. The audience arrives, takes their seats, and murmurs for some time before a bell sounds or the lights dim, which indicates that the show is about to start. A hush comes over the crowd, attention turns to the stage, and the actor walks out. The show has begun.

Think about the impact of the theater on the performance. There is a clear listener and a clear teller. Now, imagine if the acting troupe attempted to perform while everyone was having dinner and chatting. Attention would be scattered. This may seem like a completely obvious observation about context, but in fact, what we are pointing to is the quality of the listening that each context evokes. In a theater, we remember the details of shows, presentations, and so forth, because we tuned in to them. We want that same precision in our listening in the workplace. How do we create an optimal listening environment at work?

GUIDELINES FOR CREATING A DEDICATED TIME AND SPACE

What follows are guidelines for how to define a dedicated time and space for listening and storytelling, whether they happen in person or online. The seven principle guidelines are the following:

1. Why a meeting? Why now?

2. Create a dedicated time and space.

3. Manage the time.

4. Identify and release obstacles to listening and set an intention.

5. Designate dedicated listeners.

6. Instruct participants to tell what happened.

7. Record and share.

Guidline 1. Why a Meeting? Why Now?

Just as you must consider why you're choosing to tell a specific story to another person or group of people, you must be able to answer why you're calling a meeting (as opposed to using other means of communication) and why at this particular time. One of the issues with meetings is that people often relate to them as though they're on automatic pilot. They just let the plane do the work, sit back, and doze off.

Meetings can also be a knee-jerk response to chaos or uncertainty. That's where the prompt Why a meeting? Why now? comes into play: it requires that you slow down and take a moment to get clear on why you're asking for people's attention and time. You're the driver of this meeting, and you're responsible for creating an environment in which people feel heard and actively contribute to a common purpose, a business objective. Even if this is a recurring team meeting, keep asking yourself the questions: Why this meeting? Why now? By doing so, you will bring focus from start to finish. Additionally, you may avoid wasting time if the moment's truly not right for a gathering.

Guideline 2. Create a Dedicated Time and Space

You've called the meeting for a specific time and day, you've circulated an agenda, and you've let people know where to go or how to connect to the meeting. By doing this, you've activated the reciprocal relationship between listening and telling. Your meeting participants are your listeners, and you are the teller who has called for this gathering. Your priority now is to create a space for listening. Remember that listening begins with you. So think of the environment you need in order to listen to yourself and then think of who the listeners in the meeting will be. According to this, identify all the obstacles that may get in the way of the listening you are creating for this meeting. Start with the space.

Make sure that the space will remain private throughout the length of the meeting. For example, the space should not be one that people need to go through in order to get to the pantry or kitchen or copier. We once ran a meeting for a client in a room that housed the fax, printer, and copier for the entire office. As a result, we had the distraction of the machine turning on every few minutes, and people walking in to retrieve papers from the machine. We asked for permission to turn the machine off for the duration of the meeting. Everyone agreed because they recognized that this was an obstacle to listening that was preventing people from concentrating on the agenda.

Is the room big enough to accommodate everyone, or is it too big, thereby making it hard to hear when someone speaks and also creating physical distance between people?

The following is a list of additional questions to ask yourself as you prepare the space for the meeting. Think of all the obstacles that you may anticipate in relation to the space and add to this list as you see fit:

What is the noise level surrounding the room? Can the doors be closed?

Has the room been booked for an adequate amount of time? Before the meeting is over, will people be knocking on the door, saying they need the room and distracting the meeting participants?

Is there enough light in the room? Is it too bright? Do additional lights need to be brought in? Are there any sources of natural light?

What's the temperature of the room? Are you able to regulate it?

Are there phones in the room? If so, make sure they are unplugged and will not ring during the meeting.

Now think of the seating. Chairs should be arranged in such a way that every group member is able to see and be seen by all others. If you're conducting a meeting from a space where a few people are in a room and others are in front of their computer screens from a different office or their homes, make sure those in the room can all be seen by those who are connecting online. (For more on creating the space for an online meeting, see "Guidelines for Creating a Space for an Online Meeting" at the end of this section.)

Think of the creation of the space as if you were inviting people to your home for dinner. You're setting the table and paying great attention to detail because you care about your guests and you want them to feel comfortable and energized. How is this space you're creating contributing to a feeling of inclusiveness and productivity?

Similarly, what will you give your participants to ensure that their physical obstacles to listening, such as hunger and thirst, are taken care of? Make sure to have coffee, tea, water, or whatever else you think is needed to increase people's attention during the meeting. Don't leave it up to them to bring what they need or, at the very least, let people know to bring their own sustenance if you are not able to provide snacks or drinks.

Now that the space is set up, you're ready to greet your guests.

Guideline 3. Manage the Time

Most of us tend to relate to meetings as having a beginning and an end, and that's the extent of it. Instead, when we run listening and storytelling workshops, our plan is timed to the minute. We know what we need to cover when, and we pay close attention to whether we have gone over time or not so that we can adjust. We always inform the group of any adjustments. Our disciplined timekeeping creates a safe and structured environment in which people feel that they are all heard because everyone is allotted the appropriate amount of time for speaking and for comments. The same can be applied to meetings.

Have you ever had the experience of someone hogging the time in a meeting? So much so that no one else was able to get a word in? This often contributes to the feeling of a useless meeting. You may start to have participants who ask themselves: "Why am I here? Anthony's the only one who seems to be speaking. And the person running the meeting just lets him, so why should I try?" This becomes an obstacle to all the participants' listening, an obstacle that they are not able to set aside, so people start to think about their to-do list and other tasks. Now you've lost them.

To counteract that "attention loss," let people know that this meeting is going to be timed and designate a dedicated timekeeper whose role is to make sure that everyone gets the same amount of time to speak, or alternatively, you can dedicate the time proportionally based on the emphasis of the meeting.

Having a limit on time has interesting effects on presentation. This technique is borrowed from our workshops in which each participant gets to practice telling a story. If storytellers know that their story will reliably end after a certain number of minutes, they will be able to choose which elements of the story are the most important for them to communicate. It is not helpful to give people extra time, even though in the moment this may feel like the generous thing to do.

In a similar way, a time limit creates focus and precision in a meeting. As the person running the meeting, you want to let your participants know that what they have to say matters and that everyone's time is precious. So your participants need to know that they have a limited amount of time to say what they need to say. This requires them to prepare for the meeting and to know that they will be called on to speak or to comment.

The timekeeper's role is to regulate the flow of communication in the meeting so that all the participants are encouraged to get to the essence of what they need to say. In the listening and storytelling groups we run, the timekeepers always have two essential instruments: a timer and a bell that they ring when time is up. The timekeepers for your meetings can have the same instruments, or perhaps they can use an all-in-one device like a smartphone, which has a built-in timer that chimes when the time is up. The timekeepers must be discreet yet firm, and they must use their device *only* for the purpose of timekeeping, so if they're using a smartphone, they must have it on airplane mode so that nothing else triggers a sound.

When the speaker's time is up, regardless of where he or she is in the comment or its content, that's it. The timekeeper's role is to ensure that everyone knows this particular participant's time is up. It will then be up to you, as the person running the meeting, to let the participant finish a thought or wrap up in some way by guiding the speaker to the conclusion of what he or she is saying.

One of the steps we follow when excavating and crafting a story is to find our end before we present the story (see Chapter 6, "Find Your Ending"). The same principle applies for your meeting participants. When preparing people for the meeting, let them know what is expected of them. If you've tasked certain people to present, then ask them for their last line—their concluding point—before the meeting starts. This way, you know where they're going, and you'll know to guide them to that last line if they have filled up their time to speak before getting to their end. At first, this might read as if the time-keeper has an overly intrusive role or too much authority, but in fact, when the group agrees to this practice, the timekeeper's role is that of a unifier. He or she is caring for the overall shape of the meeting, which allows each person to participate fully.

Guideline 4. Identify and Release Obstacles to Listening and Set an Intention

Identify the Obstacles to Listening

When you start the meeting, go around the room and ask people to say what their obstacles to listening are in the moment.

We do this in a meeting so that everyone can become aware of what obstacles exist in people's individual listening. As the person running the meeting, you've identified the obstacles related to space and time by following guidelines 2 and 3.

Release the Obstacles to Listening

Now you have people walking into the room, and you have no idea in that moment what they're bringing to the table in terms of their mindsets. Asking them to identify their obstacles will allow everyone to check in with one another and ensure that everyone is responsible for committing to releasing their obstacles for the duration of the meeting. Remember, identifying and releasing the obstacles is not meant as suppression or rejection; it's about acknowledging and putting things aside so that everyone can get the most out of the meeting experience.

To understand the benefits of this simple practice, let's take an example. As the person running the meeting, you may open by stating the agenda of the meeting, and one person might be frowning or shifting in her seat. At that moment, this might throw you off because you are thinking to yourself, "Am I saying something that's causing this person to frown and shift in her seat? Did I say something wrong? What's happening?" Whereas if before stating the agenda you start by asking what obstacles people have in their listening, you may hear this from that same person: "I woke up with lower back pain today, and sitting down is quite uncomfortable. It's causing me to shift in my seat and to wince." Thanks to this practice, you now know that whatever you say next, that person's appearance and behavior will have nothing to do with you but everything to do with her physical obstacle to listening, that is, physical pain. By identifying their obstacles, people are also indicating that you are not responsible for their obstacles. It's up to the individuals to contend with their obstacles, not you.

Ask your timekeeper to time this part of the meeting too, so that everyone gets the same amount of time to identify his obstacles, and remember to give the instruction that no one interrupt the person who's speaking about his obstacles. This step also functions as an icebreaker in team settings. It allows people to break through whatever little bit of stage fright they may have since everyone is doing it. It would be interesting to calculate the loss to businesses in terms of efficiency incurred by people simply not speaking up.

Set an Intention

Now that everyone's identified and released his or her obstacles to listening, you have an opportunity to create a different shape of listening by setting an intention and asking everyone to do the same.

Setting an intention calls you into a certain way of being, which is not the habitual way you may have of approaching a meeting. For instance, an intention may be one word or one sentence such as "Focus" or "My intention is to listen constructively to what is said in this meeting." By stating this intention, you are indicating to everyone in the group what kind of listener you're going to be for each one of them. By asking everyone to do the same, you end up with a rich tapestry of intentions that give you a clear picture of who's in the room and what they are intending to contribute to the meeting. You would not know this if you didn't ask the question. This also has the advantage of taking only a few seconds per person.

One note about speaking and listening in a meeting: it's sometimes unrealistic to think that everyone will be speaking in a meeting, but that doesn't mean that those who aren't speaking are passive. On the contrary, in our view they are dedicated listeners, and it's important to let your participants know that that's who they are.

Guideline 5. Designate Dedicated Listeners

Coming back to the reciprocal relationship between listening and telling, it's important to acknowledge in the meeting that everyone there is first and foremost a listener for one another.

As the person running the meeting, let people know that their listening is going to shape what people say. When we run listening and storytelling workshops, we designate dedicated listeners. You can do the same in your meeting. By designating someone as a dedicated listener, you give that person a particular job for the meeting.

Her role is to listen openly, without judgment. She is also listening for the specificity of what's being said, according to the What happened? method (refer to Chapter 5 for complete instructions). By designating someone as the dedicated listener, you know that there is someone whose listening you can count on to actively support and shape what you and others are going to say.

Guideline 6. Instruct Participants to Tell What Happened

I've noticed that meetings are often seen as an opportunity for people to air their grievances about the way things are done in the business, even though that wasn't the agenda of the meeting. The result often feels like a hijacking of the meeting for the participants who aren't speaking. And for the person who's running the meeting, it's difficult to find something actionable out of what the participant is expressing because it's all about his feelings, and what can you do about the way someone feels? This is where instructing people to tell only what happened transforms and benefits the meeting as a whole.

For example, if someone says she's upset at a colleague because of the way she was treated by that person, this is an opportunity for the dedicated listener to ask the question "What happened?" and keep the person to the facts of what made her upset. Using this method, the person would not say she was upset, which is an interpretation. She would have to say only what happened. So she might say, "The other day, I was running back to my desk from a meeting with my boss, and Jack was waiting by my computer. He said, 'Well, it's about time. Were you getting a snack again?' and then he walked away and said, with his back to me, 'I left a note on your desk regarding the client meeting at 3.'"

Now that's what happened. Feelings are not necessary to interpolate into the telling because for listeners it's easy to interpret how the protagonist must have felt. But more important, it gives you and everyone else in the room an opportunity to respond with a specific and appropriate action. For instance, this could lead to your saying, "That sounds like an HR issue. I recommend you take that up with so-and-so from HR, and I'll be happy to support you." Or, "I'd like to set up a meeting between you and Jack so that you have an opportunity to tell him the impact on you of what he said." Whatever you decide to do with the information is your business, but the point is that you know what happened so you can act accordingly, and the situation doesn't have to derail your meeting.

Always ask What happened? no matter what the content of your communications. It will transform the way your meetings sound and affect their outcomes too, because it will force you to identify and take out what is unnecessary—that is, your opinions, assumptions, interpretations, and feelings about a situation. Everyone ends up dealing with the same basic information. In meetings, this means that you can use the What happened? method to refine your message to others and get to the heart of the matter concisely. In short, it's an editing tool for you to make your point more quickly and in a more straightforward way.

This requires that everyone be on the same page in terms of how they communicate, which is why you need dedicated listeners who can question people when they are straying from What happened? Just as we ask questions to further thicken a story—that is, substantiating it with greater detail—you and your dedicated listeners can ask questions that help the speakers drive their point forward. But do *not* ask "Why?" This is not about motives. The question must begin with "What?" You would *not* ask, "Why did you choose not to stop Jack in his tracks and confront him?" That would be a question of motive and interpretation, and it would not be useful for this exercise. Rather, you might ask: "What happened after Jack left?" "Did you call him?" "What was your reply?" "What did you do then?"

By keeping the story in the factual realm, we reduce the mental clutter of so many interpretations and judgments. You can feel the temperature dropping in the discussion, and each listener feels there's room for his or her own insights. Otherwise, conversations based on pre-conceptions inevitably only kick up dust.

Guideline 7. Record and Share

This final guideline is critical. Always record your meetings. I don't mean that you need to have an audio or video recorder on at all times (although that is what we do in our listening and storytelling workshops, so I highly recommend it if you have time to transcribe these recordings, which may not always be practical).

I mean "recording" in the basic sense of the term. Make sure what is said is recorded, whether through precise note-taking or through an electronic device. Designate someone to take notes and to share those notes with everyone.

The note taker must be able to highlight the important What happened? details of the meeting itself, that is, the actions that were decided on and who will be accountable for those actions. We use a number of communication tools to share who's accountable for what so that we can keep track of the actions that were decided on during the meeting. Choose one that works for you.

GUIDELINES FOR LISTENING AND FEEDBACK

In keeping with our storytelling methodology, we have developed the following principles for how to give feedback from a place of open listening:

- Feedback is always a comment on the *content* and never on the *teller*.

- Feedback is *not* an evaluation, judgment, interpretation, or opinion. Rather, it is meant to elicit clarification from the teller about what happened.

All feedback begins with an *acknowledgment* of what works. It is always possible to find something that works about something that someone just shared. Providing immediate acknowledgment is an effective way of maintaining the speaker's listening, as it helps to assuage the evaluative or self-critical inner voice.

Feedback relates to how effectively the speakers followed the rule of saying what happened and also how closely what the speakers said relates to the topics and agenda you've set for the meeting. Then identify points for improvement by showing them where they strayed from the topics, agenda, or the What happened? in their statements.

When you follow this disciplined approach to feedback, you support the entire concept of a dedicated time and space in which attention is highly focused and communication is precise. There's always time to follow up outside the practice space, and its benefits will show up in the communication you have afterward.

GUIDELINES FOR CREATING THE SPACE FOR AN ONLINE MEETING

It is a different experience to listen via video chat than to listen in person. Your computer is an actual space. It is home to your e-mails, photos, music, and many other personal programs and documents. Due to the number of distractions that exist in this space, it requires extra focus to remain engaged when you are staring at a computer screen. Additionally, because we are all in separate physical spaces, each individual may be experiencing different distractions than are other members in the group. We want to bring attention to the computer as a space so that we can be aware of the potential distractions and do what we can beforehand to create our own individual spaces as environments in which to listen during a meeting.

Here is a checklist of recommended actions and practices that can help you create an optimal environment for participating in a meeting online:

- Make sure that you get to your computer with enough time to set up your space, log in, and download materials.

- Silence your electronic devices and put them away for the duration of the meeting.

- Minimize or close all windows and applications on your computer except for the meeting window.

- Turn off notifications and pop-ups, such as calendar reminders, e-mail, and chat notifications.

- Make a commitment to not look at other windows or the Internet on your computer. We know the computer is a work space, but we are transforming it into a meeting space.

- If your Internet connection drops or if there is a feed delay, don't stress. Work out what you have to, then rejoin the meeting when you can.

- What will we see when we see you? Choose a place with something in the background that reflects you.

- Find a private space. Close doors if possible and eliminate any external noises that the group might be able to hear in your background.

- Try to find a light source on your face instead of sitting in a backlit area so the group can see you.

- Tell the people who share your physical space about the meeting and ask not to be interrupted for the duration of the meeting.

- Make a commitment to deal with your own distractions and obstacles as they arise; the group will not necessarily experience your obstacles because you are not together.

- Take care of any food, drink, and nourishment that you need.

Feel free to add additional items to this list if you feel it helps you create the optimal environment you need for the meeting.

CASE STUDY: TECH STARTUP

Let's look at a case in which Narativ was hired by a tech startup to address communication conflicts that were manifesting as a breakdown of their meeting culture, evidenced by this comment from a senior manager: "I always leave meetings with a headache."

The startup's management team agreed that the objective of meetings was to increase productivity through clear and purposeful communication and that the best way to achieve this was by knowing what the goals were for each meeting and coming prepared. Yet meetings kept breaking down due to a number of persistent obstacles to listening. Important stories were not being heard, great ideas were overlooked, and there was a widespread loss of engagement. When they talked about these problems, they never arrived at any satisfactory or lasting solutions. They asked Narativ to take the team on a one-day listening and storytelling retreat to address these issues. In other words, they sought a dedicated time and space with the specific intention of addressing communication breakdowns.

As we sat with them at the retreat, we heard, "There's a norm of not listening and a belief that multitasking is synonymous with productivity." We observed that practices had seeped into their culture that were not conducive to productive communication. At this company, everyone gets a laptop, which they bring to every meeting. The general attitude had become, "If everyone else is on their computer, constantly checking their phones, and engaging in side conversations, why can't I be too?"

When people are taking notes on a laptop, it can often feel as though they are not listening. And they're constantly being distracted by notifications that pop up on-screen. Conversations about technology often reveal an issue of time scarcity: "Meetings take up too much time. They're useless if there isn't time to prepare. Time is money. How do you use time efficiently? Well, you might as well work during the meeting."

One of the managers argued that it's reassuring to be on your laptop in what's perceived to be an inefficient meeting. "At least I'm doing something productive." Another expressed her relationship to meetings and technology as a feeling of panic: "I am not going to be able to do everything I need to, so I work during the presentation." In our culture, working fast, thinking about a lot of different things, and always being connected have indeed become synonymous with productivity: "That's why smart people can conquer!" Clearly the technology itself was not an obstacle. Instead, what became apparent in the intimate environment of this retreat were a number of fears:

> **Fear of getting it wrong:** People thought that they should have a solution to present if they had a criticism: "For me, it's a fear of being challenged on an opinion that I don't have a developed reason for." "I'm not confident in what to say. I fear criticism, so I just accommodate."

Fear of taking the lead: "I'm always wondering if it's up to me to say what's productive and not." People felt that the CEO had the vision and they should just buy into it and go with it.

Fear of missing out: "I'm caught in a perpetual Catch-22. Meetings take a lot of time, and most of the time, they don't need me there, so I don't engage. The reason I don't challenge the invite is because I don't want to feel I missed something. It's hard to let go."

Fear of repercussions: "I've got a fear and anxiety that if I challenge someone in the meeting, it will follow me out of this room back to the office. I'm afraid if I speak up, I'll be labeled and not truly understood."

In addition, there were *relational* and *psychological (emotional) obstacles* that prevented the team from saying what needed to be said. There was a loss of honesty and transparency. Conversations seemed not to have the right substance. The company's CEO observed that the biggest issue was the power dynamics. "Where there's power, there's also fear," he told us. "What might be expressed as kindness and respect for each other could really be that we are holding back from saying important things because we're afraid of repercussions. Even caretaking can actually be a way of avoiding discomfort."

In this listening section of our training, many layers of obstacles became apparent, from the obvious and superficial to the more subtle and invasive. Listening, it turns out, is a kind of sonar: it picks up all kinds of information. In a dedicated time and space, such as this retreat environment, listening naturally prepares for storytelling to take place. But in this instance, we first had to unearth obstacles to listening and then employ storytelling to release and address them.

To fully identify and release the obstacles that were bubbling up, we suggested that each member of the management team simply tell the story of what happened: what had led to the communication breakdown? In their responses, we heard stories of fear, of misinterpretation, of judgment, of confusion, of collaboration. The variety of stories was remarkable. Equally so was the quality of the listening that took place. More than just "feeling heard" in this session, the leadership team found a new cohesion and inspiration to move ahead.

FEELINGS AS AN OBSTACLE TO LISTENING

Many people ask, "If I am upset about something, how do I let it go?" In other words, what if your obstacles involve strong emotions, especially about team members? For example, someone said something that hurt you. This is where the practice of identifying and releasing obstacles to listening gains real traction by revealing the kind of culture you have at your company. Is it one that values tolerance and acceptance of the full range of human experience as integral to the workplace, or does it draw a line that suggests emotions are best left at home?

The Narativ method of listening and telling embraces challenging emotions and situations with honesty and bravery. Can we listen to something hard and put our reaction aside? What benefit accrues from this behavior for ourselves and our teammates? Bonds are at stake. We fear they might be broken, but more often than not, this practice enhances camaraderie and provides internal relief to accumulated tensions with coworkers. It breeds understanding and empathy that mitigate resentment and division. Bringing the human dimension back into the workplace can spark creative freedom and reduce archaic belief systems that inhibit it.

How do we apply the Narativ method in a situation in which strong emotions are involved? First, release by speaking the obstacle as your story. Use the What happened? method to relate just the facts without interpretation and opinion (see Chapter 5). Then literally take a breath and exhale. Let it go. The question is not whether you can put challenging feelings away forever, but rather, can you put them on a shelf and not in the space of the storytelling just for today? See what happens if you do. This is one of the powers of storytelling. To tell *past* our fear and listen *past* our reaction. And then, most important, move forward to the business at hand.

Here is a summary of the ground rules to follow when releasing obstacles to listening. Again, these are premised on having a dedicated time and space with a clear intention:

1. Let each person in the group express what his or her obstacles are individually. It's essential for everyone to get a turn. Set a time limit for each person, according to how much time has been allocated to do this exercise, so that all are heard.

2. We don't interrupt, comment on, or otherwise interject any of our own thoughts, beliefs, or feelings when someone else is in the middle of speaking his or her obstacles with the group. We're simply creating space to note the presence of the obstacles and to let them go. We wait for our turn to speak before we identify our own obstacles.

3. We thank the person who has just identified his
   or her obstacles and then move on to the next.

STORYTELLING
AND CHANGE

Change means letting go of old stories and creating new
ones or finding new ways to tell a story. One of the most
surprising (and counterintuitive) ways of releasing your
obstacles to listening is by offering to listen to someone's
story, openly and without judgment. All you have to do
is ask, "What happened?" After that, relax and enjoy
the story. Yes, obstacles will begin to get in your way.
You may think of something you need to do later in the
day, so you lose track of the story at that moment. Bring
yourself back by observing the obstacle and then letting
it go from your mind. This is achieved by directing your
breathing. First notice your breath, how you inhale and
exhale. Allow the obstacle to be released as you exhale.
Let it be carried away by the out breath. It releases stress
and provides pleasure.

As a neurological function, storytelling undoes the
animal fight-or-flight responses that linger in our primitive brains, the fight-or-flight brain that tells us that we've
got to keep talking, make a noise, be noticed, be heard.

Even when we're not talking out loud, we're talking to ourselves. How is it possible to discern anything with all that interior and exterior noise?

Of course, there are times when identifying and releasing will not work. When teams are not aligned in their goals. When the majority of people do not care. So this work is for teams that share a passion and focus and want to improve communication or bring it back after it's gone astray. Listening and storytelling in an organization take leadership as much as they take commitment from participants. It needn't be a time-consuming indulgence or emotional smorgasbord. Actually, it's quite the opposite. It's putting all of that aside and simply clearing the decks for productivity in a mutually respectful and productive way.

WAYS TO RELEASE OBSTACLES TO LISTENING

Table 3.1 lists examples of situations that lead to obstacles and how we might address them.

TABLE 3.1	Sample Obstacles and Ways to Release Them	
Categories of Obstacles to Listening	Examples	Ways to Release Obstacles
External	"There's a construction crew outside with a jackhammer."	Close all windows. Find another room to work from. Ask the crew how long the jackhammer will be going, and if it's not going to be a long time, take a break away from the construction site.
Physical	"I'm so hungry, I can't listen."	Get food! If that's not practical, ask for a break and get a power bar. Even better, next time carry a power bar with you if you know this tends to happen.
Internal	"I'm so angry at John for stealing my idea."	Write this down, or tell someone you trust and ask that person to listen to you. See what that does to the feeling of anger. Does it exacerbate it? Does it reduce it? Do you need to talk to John?
Psychological	"My boss is so intimidating. I don't think I'll ever be able to stand up for myself."	Notice the judgment of yourself. Write it down or speak to someone and don't judge it. Ask yourself: "What would 'standing up for myself' look *(continued)*

Categories of Obstacles to Listening	Examples	Ways to Release Obstacles
Psychological *(continued)*		like? What would I do? What have I got to gain from not standing up for myself? What have I got to lose by standing up for myself? Is there an action I can take to releases this obstacle, or is this something I need to let go?"
Relational	"My director of research always cuts off other people on my team."	Note the obstacle or tell it to someone. Actions you can take to address this obstacle: Speak to the director of research and ask him or her to practice more awareness of others. Describe the impact his or her interruptions have on the team. Encourage your team to speak up when interruptions occur. Ask your team if they perceive your director of research the same way. Ask yourself what there is to gain or lose from actions you can take.

Now take a moment to fill out the middle column of Table 3.2 to see if any new obstacles have emerged since the last chapter. Use the right-most column to make notes as you check in with yourself, note the obstacles, and see what questions you need to ask, what actions you need to take, and what you need to let go. Also write down the ways you will address these obstacles so that you can release them instead of being driven by them.

TABLE 3.2 **My Obstacles to Listening and How to Release Them**		
Categories of Obstacles to Listening	**My Obstacles Are . . .**	**Ways to Release Obstacles (Actions, Questions, People to Speak To)**
External		
Physical		
Internal		
Psychological		
Relational		

The benefits of an optimal listening environment are innumerable. It's like clearing the playing field. Here are some of the benefits we've routinely observed:

- Teams can capture good ideas. In the preface, I mentioned that I've never seen anyone too shy to tell a story. This is because the practice of releasing obstacles allows people to express what's truly there, without fear of judgment or criticism. That breeds creativity, and that's how you can capture ideas from the most unlikely team members.

- In an optimal listening environment, teams can identify hidden problems or issues. In contrast, the proverbial elephant in the room can be easily obscured if everyone is checking text messages or answering e-mails during a meeting.

- Listening after obstacles have been identified can help teams work through interpersonal conflict. Story can be a way to objectively portray what happened that led to a conflict or misunderstanding so that both parties can come to greater clarity and resolution.

- Story can help teams create connection and empathy. When you hear someone else say he is worried about his child at daycare and he misses his child, this likely will trigger a sense of connection if you have had a similar experience. Even if you haven't had it, hearing it will trigger empathy and give you a perspective on that person that you didn't have before.

- Team members can recognize and appreciate their fellow team members' unique voices, styles, and contributions.

Up to this point, we have been speaking about identifying and releasing obstacles to listening as a group practice in preparation for storytelling (or any type of group communication). However, identifying and releasing can be an internal practice we do on our own when we are excavating a story that we will tell in an upcoming meeting or conference. To apply this practice internally, follow this process:

1. Identify your audience.

2. Identify obstacles.

3. Release obstacles.

4. Tell what happened.

Let's look closely at how we begin. What does it mean to identify your audience when it's just you? This simply means to internalize your anticipated audience for the purposes of identifying obstacles and releasing them. For example, you are preparing a story for a sales meeting. Imagine the meeting: the time, the place, the room, and who will be attending. What obstacles arise for you? What's "in your listening" about that environment? Does fear arise because a senior manager will be there? Are you a bit uncomfortable speaking in public? Are you trying to wish away some uncertainties about the business plan you will be talking about?

Such rich material! Release it. By bringing it to your awareness, you are releasing it in the sense that you are freeing it to be present in your mind rather than suppressing it. To do so almost always changes our relationship to the obstacles. In addition, it prepares the stage. We know what we might encounter when we begin to tell our story. It's a bit like learning how to swim and then being in the open ocean. Our training will kick in. In the context of the Narativ method, that means, having cleared the ground, you're more prepared to tell a powerful story unequivocally, forcefully, convincingly.

Additionally, we've found that the practice of identifying your audience is a shrewd tool for improving communication. So often we speak from what we know, but this might not always be what our audience wants to hear. Putting our audience in our listening sensitizes us to their interests and needs and can, in turn, shape our storytelling. It's anticipating the container, which in turn shapes the liquid. We might end up telling an entirely different story from the one we first had planned.

When developing a story, we move from identifying and releasing obstacles to telling what happened, which is described in Chapter 5. As this book is an instruction in the entire theory and practice of our method, in between the steps of releasing obstacles and telling what happened, we introduce a powerful means to engage in storytelling in an immediate way, the Grandparent Exercise. This is an exercise we use at all of our trainings that gives participants the entire experience of storytelling in just three minutes! That may sound daunting, but you'll find it's entirely enjoyable.

The grandparent exercise bridges the gap between excavating and crafing. It shows how identifying and releasing obstacles to listening prepare the ground for gathering the elements you'll be crafting into a story.

4

REMEMBER YOUR HERITAGE

My name is George McWilliams, and I was born in 1861 as an enslaved person. I don't remember much about emancipation, but I do remember hearing the bells ringing, the church bells. And I do remember someone coming in our yard wearing a white vest and telling us that we were free. And I do remember hearing one of my half-sisters say that when the master asked her to come and work in the fields, she said, "Tell Old Bartholomew he should go work his own farm now."

I grew up very poor. I had a lot of sisters and brothers, but I had this ambition that I was going to get land, and somehow I did. I was able to put together a farm piece by piece, like 50 acres here, 50 acres there. I met my wife, whose name was Mary Harvey, at the Sunday school because there were no schools for us as free people. But on Sunday she would go to the church, and they taught us to read, write, and sing.

So I met my wife there, and we ended up having 15 children. We had 8 girls and 7 boys, and my goal was to leave 100 acres of land to each one of my children. I worked hard. And I did other things. At one point, I had a cotton gin so that we could gin the cotton. I actually made bricks too. We set up this little factory, and we made bricks. And I believed in self-sufficiency, so on this farm there were chickens and ducks, and I planted an orchard.

This rich, first-person tale of a slave's transition to freedom was told not at a seminar on historical memory, not at a family gathering, but spontaneously at one of our workshops. It emerged from the Grandparent Exercise.

THE GRANDPARENT EXERCISE

It's odd how some of the most enduring practices arise from the most frustrating circumstances. I created this exercise as a direct response to resistance I encountered during my work with clients at the Brooklyn AIDS Day Program. I was searching for a storytelling practice that would simultaneously break the ice and allow people in the group to get to know one another in a substantive

manner. When I invited them to tell first-person stories about their parents, the idea backfired. The patients
seethed with anger, pain, and rage. Many group members
were gay, had been in trouble with the law, and/or had
been or still were drug addicts. As a result, most had no
relationship with their parents; many had been thrown
out of their homes. Psychiatrist C. G. Jung compared
psychotherapy to alchemy, in which one applies heat to
transform chemical elements. Too much heat and the
compound burns; too little and nothing happens. Since
the parent stories were so hot, I turned down the heat.

I asked them to tell a first-person story about a
grandparent. This proved highly effective because most
people have fond memories of their grandparents. The
Grandparent Exercise became a powerful way of locat-
ing the personal story within a larger historical context
in an intimate and emotional way.

There are two roles that are essential to conducting
this exercise:

1. The facilitator, who explains and leads the
   exercise

2. The timekeeper, whose role is not only to keep
   time but also to support the facilitator in creating the listening space for the grandparent stories
   to emerge

Here's how we explain the Grandparent Exercise to participants in our workshops:

In this listening exercise, the group will be giving and receiving the *gift of listening* to each person, and even when there are obstacles to listening, each group member will bring his or her listening back to the person who is speaking.

You will notice that we haven't asked you to introduce yourselves. The first thing you do when you meet someone is introduce yourself and tell him or her what your profession or other life role is. Here we purposefully did not ask you to do that, and now we are going to ask you to introduce yourself, but not as yourself. We are going to ask you to introduce yourself as one of your grandparents. And when I say introduce yourself, I mean really become that person, so speak in the first person: "My name is . . . "

The facilitator will be attuned to the effect that these instructions have on the listening of individuals in the group. People are probably shifting in their seats and wondering which grandparent they should choose. Very often it happens that people didn't know their grandparents, and that's fine. If you have any memory, a photograph, anything at all that someone else said about that grandparent, draw on that image.

When running this group exercise, we refer to the work of anthropologist and filmmaker Barbara Myerhoff, who used the term "re-membering" as a way of ritually including deceased persons into the current time and place.[1] We can see life as a membered club. When people die, they lose their membership. Telling a story about them is a way of bringing them back to life. Re-membering them. This is what we do by listening to and telling stories about our grandparents.

THE GROUND RULES

Our workshop instructions continued:

> You will have three minutes to present yourself as your grandparent. Speak in the first person "I" point of view, tell us your name, and somewhere in the course of the story, tell us when you were born and whether you are currently alive or have died. If you have died, please tell us when.
>
> Please remember that this exercise is really about listening. It is not about performance or delivery. It's about the listening, which is the

safe container for your story and which will also shape the story that you tell. You may think that you can prepare for this, but once you start speaking, the listening will take you in directions you cannot predict. In this group, you can speak anything. You will have three minutes each to tell your story. After three minutes, we will ring a bell and your time will be up. Remember, it is the listening that creates the telling.

At this point, participants are reminded to put away any pens or papers they may have. The timekeeper times each participant and rings the bell after three minutes. After each grandparent story is told, the teller is asked to give the story a name, and the facilitator writes the story title and the teller's name on a flip chart.

The facilitator neither comments on the content of the story nor offers any suggestions for story improvement. The only comment made to the storyteller is a warm, genuine "Thank you." After each story, the facilitator asks the group, "How was your listening? Were there any obstacles?"

People may respond, "I was thinking about my story," or "I was thinking about how little I know about my grandparents."

The facilitator acknowledges these obstacles by responding with, "You are now aware you have an obstacle because you have spoken it. You have acknowledged that it is there. Now let it go, hit the refresh button as you would on a computer, and bring yourself back to be fully present for the next story."

The facilitator then moves on to the next person.

If some people appear to be distracted, the facilitator may specifically ask them to reflect on their obstacles to listening. If someone—the storyteller or any of the listeners—starts to cry or becomes emotional, that's fine. There's no need to comfort or coddle anyone. There's no limit to how long or how frequent the post-story listening reflections should be. The facilitator's job is to move the energy in the circle and make certain that everyone in the group understands the rules and feels safe.

After a while, the facilitator may decide to acknowledge the group's listening and move on to the next story by saying, "Well done with the listening. Who is next?" If a story has been particularly emotional or painful, the facilitator can invite the group to take a collective breath as a way of letting go of the previous story and moving on to the next one. It is also important to acknowledge the group for the level of their listening and share that you think they are doing a good job of listening.

After the last story is told, thank everyone for giving the gift of listening to one another and congratulate participants for being present and bringing powerful listening to the circle.

When we use this exercise with teams, it provides a means of connecting people to a sense of where they come from and simultaneously sharing that bit of background with their teammates. Liberated from the pressure to talk intimately about themselves, which is horribly uncomfortable for some, participants are nonetheless able to share a deeply personal relationship. For a group, the exercise creates a sense of unity in that having grandparents—whether or not one has ever known them—is a universal phenomenon. It naturally stimulates our sense of empathy and understanding.

As Craig Kostelic of Condé Nast told us, "The Grandparent Exercise put me in my grandmother's shoes, how life was through her eyes, what she thinks her life represented, and the things that she went through. I think we largely look at our grandparents as symbols of something rather than actual people. Talking about her life as if I were her made a huge difference. It humanized her in my eyes."

In the context of the Narativ method, the Grandparent Exercise demonstrates the following:

- That there is a reciprocal relationship between listening and telling

- That listening is a gift

- That everyone has a story

- That everyone is equipped to tell a story

- That basic storytelling principles can be applied by anyone

- That a story can be constructed with fragments of memory and information

- And that however much you protest you can't tell a story, you'll find it's a natural ability of your brain!

As we mentioned already, when we conduct the Grandparent Exercise in our workshops for companies, we ask people to introduce themselves as one of their grandparents, and we give them three minutes to do so. The moment we give that instruction, people's brains start to engage with storytelling. They remember an instant with their grandparent, something that happened that made an impact on them, and then they tell it without any preparation. As they tell their story about their grandparent as their grandparent, people who are listening lean in and give their full attention because their brains are now fully engaged in storytelling.

Think back to the opening story of this chapter: What happened to you when you read it? How did it impact you? What memories came up for you? What parts of your experience were engaged by that story? Did it make you think of your own grandparents? What were their circumstances? How might you tell their story if you were given three minutes to do so?

Now try the Grandparent Exercise in your work environment and experience its impact. The exercise is not simply a warm-up to storytelling. It can be implemented to reach communication goals in and of itself.

Let's look at a case study in which the Grandparent Exercise was used to powerful effect in bringing a global leadership team together for the first time with the goal of collaboration and connection.

The HR director of a major media entertainment company e-mailed me after seeing my storytelling performance *Two Men Talking*. She was "compelled" by how my childhood friend and cofounder of Narativ Paul Browde and I listened and told stories to each other onstage. Our program said we ran storytelling workshops for companies. She wanted to meet.

One week later I was in her office facing a giant map of the world dotted with red pushpins on India, Russia, China, South Africa, Israel, Iran, Turkey, Singapore, Greece, and other countries. She told me she was putting together a conference where leaders from these countries, 40 in all, would gather.

Next thing I knew, I was on the phone with a senior vice president at their Paris headquarters. "We're all about magic," said he, "and that's what I want to create." This conference was a very rare opportunity for managers from around the world to meet one another, in most cases for the first time. He wanted something spectacular that would "break down boundaries among people." He cautioned that some participants were from countries that had waged wars against each other and whose governments still hated one another. "I have just the thing," I said, and I told him about the Grandparent Exercise.

He chose Cyprus for the conference, a global midpoint where East meets West. I flew to Paphos and checked into my hotel.

The next morning the senior vice president introduced me as a storytelling guru. One hundred sixty curious faces looked at me. At the midmorning tea, he gave me the thumbs-up. My introduction had been pitch perfect. Everyone had loved my story, even the listening contemplation. While we chatted, hotel staff rapidly arranged the chairs in two large circles, one inside the other, all seats facing the center. Lists were posted assigning people to the inner or outer circle.

When we returned to the room, the noise level rose as people looked at the circles and wondered why they'd been assigned to one or the other. I was fitted with a headset mic, and my voice boomed out across the enormous room.

There was hushed silence as I explained that the outside circle consisted of company "old-timers" who mostly knew one another. The inner circle comprised those who were relatively new. Then I gave the instruction: all those in the inner circle would present themselves as one of their four grandparents in the first person, using the pronoun *I*. There was a three-minute time limit, and I would ring a bell when the time was up. The only job of the outer circle was to listen openly without criticism or judgment.

There was an audible collective gasp. "Who's first?" I asked looking around the inner circle.

The first was an Iranian woman who channeled her grandmother, who never went to school, was sold into marriage at the age of 11, was widowed at 16, was sold again into marriage, and had nine children. Midway through the story, she began to sob. The women on either side of her put their arms around her and gave her tissues.

"Your emotions are welcome here," I reassured her. "There's no need to fear or judge them. They are part of life, part of telling stories. Emotions are the release valves for stories that are painful and hard to tell," I explained. "She's okay," I said to her coworkers. "There's no need to take care of her." When she finished, I thanked her. She wiped the tears from her cheeks.

Next was a woman from Belgium. She told the story of her grandmother, who had scavenged from garbage cans during World War II, doing anything to feed her children. She too cried, and I once again promised that feelings and emotions were permitted.

The third teller was a Polish woman, who incarnated her grandfather, a poor farmer. Conscripted as a soldier at the age of 21, he left his pregnant wife to go to war—and never returned. Once again there were tears.

After checking in with the teller, I turned to the audience in the two circles to check in with their listening. "What are your obstacles to listening?" I asked, looking at the outer circle. Before anyone could answer, a man stood up and said, "I'm from Germany. Let's face it, when I say that my grandparents were Nazis, you all know what I am talking about. I am not at all comfortable talking about this."

A man from the Netherlands spoke: "It's mostly the women who are crying. They're too emotional. This is not how to conduct yourself at work." Another man concurred: "This is the reason that women don't get far in business. They don't know how to be professional."

The senior vice president stood. "If I had known this was what you were going to do, I would never have agreed to this! You are upsetting these people." His voice grew louder. "And I don't like to see my people upset."

I asked if there were any further obstacles to listening. There was silence. I turned to him: "May I continue?"

And he replied, "You might as well."

By the end of that morning, we had traveled across the globe listening to 60 grandparent stories: soldiers, sailors, nurses, farmers, housemaids, mothers with multiple children, poets, musicians, and merchants. Over the next two days, we listened to many reflections about the Grandparent Exercise. The Indian team members were unanimous in feeling that the exercise was a precious opportunity to honor their ancestors in front of their colleagues. The Iranian woman cherished seeing her grandmother in a new light, and she felt gratitude for the good fortune of her own freedom and the opportunity to work with this team. While many said it was the most powerful training they'd ever attended, others felt it was an invasion of their privacy, that it was too touchy-feely and too American. A man from Italy said, "I don't come to work to find meaning. I am there to fill the shareholders' pockets. My family is where I find meaning, not my work."

Finally, while standing in the passport control line at the airport in Larnaca, a participant from Singapore tapped me on the shoulder. "That was quite an experience," he said. "You must be exhausted."

I asked for his reflections. He took a moment and said, "You placed a golden thread through our hearts in a very mystical way."

Ten years later, as part of the research for this book I wrote to one of the company's regional directors, who had attended the Cyprus training. I asked what he re-membered.

He told me that in all his years at the company, it was one of the most memorable trainings, but it was also the most controversial. He explained that until Narativ, the emerging markets group had done very standard, common trainings regarding planning, selling, and basic communication. Nothing had been groundbreaking or innovative. This was very different. He said, "I think it was a right moment and a right setting. You applied the right tools for people to loosen up. Quite a few people were surprised by themselves, that they had been so open and spontaneous and transparent."

"Why had it been so controversial?" I asked.

"We had never been pushed outside of our comfort zones before. It had always been easy to find our way back after the exercise. But this was more complex and a hell of a lot deeper. What we experienced was a lot of emotions in that team, which no one expected to be re-leased. However, it was clear that the individual partic-ipants each had a choice in how to present themselves."

He continued, "We were a completely new team. I think the exercise helped us to bond. By reflecting on each other's backgrounds and each other's history, we had to take into account that we all come from very different parts of the world, different cultures, with different per-sonal experiences of those. That led us to make closer connections at the outset of our conference, and over-all, I think it helped us to communicate in a better way."

Storytelling has the power to transform. Some of that power lies in how it restructures our communication through our becoming aware of the reciprocal relationship between listening and telling. Some comes from the stories themselves. Stories offer us a bridge to a new relationship with our colleagues at work. Stories dimensionalize us. They peel back layers and expose universality. They can play an evolutionary role in any team's connectivity as well as their ongoing productive relationships.

If I could prescribe one type of communication-enhancing formula for every company, it would be that every employee do the Grandparent Exercise in the presence of his or her teammates. I guarantee you that this will transform communication in each and every team.

5

TELL WHAT HAPPENED

When I met Victoria, she was wearing a black-and-white houndstooth check coat. Her lipstick, fingernails, handbag, and stilettos were all the same shade of bright red. Through long, dark lashes she made direct eye contact. She told me that she was the chief financial officer of a Bay Area technology startup "that was in a tight financial state." Personnel had been notified that "there would be layoffs" and that the "company may have to close its doors forever."

Victoria had just returned from Hong Kong, where she had met with business school friends who now worked at the Bank of Paris. She managed to obtain from her friends the venture capital needed to allow the company to keep going.

The company's leadership team had agreed that Victoria should give the toast at the annual Christmas party in the ballroom of a downtown New York City hotel. Standing at the podium and looking at 200 familiar faces, she began to hyperventilate. Her skin felt hot and cold simultaneously. She was afraid that if she said too much, she would burst into tears and make a fool of herself in front of everyone. All she managed was to raise her glass and cheer: "It was a tough year, but we made it!"

Although everyone cheered loudly and balloons were released from the ceiling, her heart sank. She'd just blown a powerful moment as a company leader to give an inspiring message. She told me, "I had something to say, and I just couldn't say it."

Victoria told me that she had a terror of public performance. Her fear prevented her from speaking from her heart.

I asked her what story she would tell if she were speaking from the heart. She didn't know where to begin.

Just saying how proud she was of the company and how hard everyone had worked brought her to tears. The company had given her a sense of purpose, belonging, and community. With fear as a listening obstacle, she "had no idea" how to talk about these things.

I asked her to tell me a story about her fear, perhaps something from her childhood.

With the right kind of curiosity and listening, we can be encouraged to tell childhood stories even when they're unresolved or painful. These stories are often defining moments in our lives that we remember long after they happened. Sharing childhood stories is a powerful way of breaking down the defensive walls we build up to protect ourselves.

These walls often continue into adulthood and impede our job performance, usually in subtle ways. In this case, as you will see, being able to tell her story allowed Victoria to rebound from this missed opportunity for leadership.

According to Narativ's method, a story is always an answer to the question "What happened?" The method provides a guideline for how to answer this question by instructing the teller to relate only facts that can be *seen, heard, tasted, touched, or smelled.* Anything else that takes place outside of the five senses, such as interpretation, opinion, commentary, judgment, thought, feeling, or emotion, does not belong in a What happened? description. The best way to demonstrate how the What happened? method affects storytelling is to continue with Victoria's telling and how I guided her using this principle:

MURRAY: What happened?

VICTORIA: I had a traumatic childhood.

M: That's not what happened. That's an interpretation. If I say "trauma" and you say "trauma," we are referring to completely different histories and facts. Simply tell me what happened. What would I have seen, touched, tasted, smelled, and heard?

V: You would have seen me sitting at the piano from the age of five.

M: What kind of piano? What color?

I am inviting Victoria to paint a visual, sensory picture:

V: It was a Kawai black baby grand. My parents gave it to me for my fifth birthday. They woke me up and told me to come into the living room. And there it was.

M: What happened then?

V: I was really excited.

M: That's a feeling. What happened? What did you do after you first saw the piano?

V: I sat down and played.

M: What did you play?

V: Hmm . . . I can't remember. What was I studying at the time? Wait . . . it was a Bach prelude and fugue. Bach's 16th Prelude and Fugue from *The Well-Tempered Clavier.*

Now that Victoria's sensory memory has been engaged, notice how the details float up to the surface of her con-sciousness, becoming more readily available and flowing more easily:

M: What happened then?

V: My piano teacher's name was Ada Gang. *Gang* in Chinese means "hard" or "rigid." And that's exactly how she was. She was very strict.

M: "Strict" is an interpretation. What would I have seen or heard?

V: She would slap my hand and call me an idiot when I played a wrong note or used the wrong fingering.

M: What did your parents say?

V: They asked me if I wanted to change teachers, but I said no because Miss Gang told me I was very talented and that I'd go far.

M: What happened then?

V: She put my name in for a piano competition. I won the prize, which was playing Mozart's 21st piano concerto with the Hong Kong Symphony.

M: What happened next?

V: I practiced for eight hours every day.

M: That's a bit abstract. What would I have seen?

V: You would have seen me sitting at my piano playing the same bars repeatedly for eight hours a day.

M: Cut to the next thing I would have seen.

V: When it was my turn to play at the competition, I came onstage to a lot of applause. I shook hands with the lead violinist, but I didn't look at her or at the audience. I was petrified.

M: Petrified is a feeling. What did you experience in your body?

V: My heart was beating so quickly. I looked down at my red dress and my red shoes. The orchestra started playing the first movement. My hands were soaked with perspiration. I was having a hard time breathing, as if my throat was closing up.

M: What happened then?

V: I woke up in the hospital. My mother was holding my hand. She told me I had collapsed.

M: What happened then?

V: I never played in front of an audience again.

Fainting in a concert hall in front of hundreds of people and a full orchestra is enough to make anyone fear public speaking. I suggested that Victoria tell this particular What happened? story to her colleagues.

A week later, Victoria gathered her colleagues together at lunchtime and told them this story, explaining why she'd become "tongue-tied" during her speech. Afterward, Victoria said that telling this story completely transformed the way people in the company saw her.

People told her that they'd previously found her to be cold, clinical, and unapproachable, but once she told that story, they could understand and empathize with her.

Before we talk about the outcome of this story for Victoria, take a moment to reflect upon what you read. How did the training session affect you as Victoria moved from interpretive, abstract statements to factual detail? Did you notice slight changes in your engagement or responsiveness? This almost biological response (in fact, according to scientific studies, this *is* precisely a neurological phenomenon) is a common experience when listening to a What happened? story. Without the filter of interpretation or commentary, you are there, in the story, alongside the teller. Your brain literally mirrors the experience of the teller, allowing for a much closer connection than is possible with other types of communication.

For Victoria, and her audience of listeners, her story became a stepping stone in her leadership. She painted a visceral portrait of the experiences that were integral to her background as the CFO of a disruptive company. She let her team get a taste of her own success and failure.

And she showed her human side, of which vulnerability and great strength are both a part. This message was critical for her team during the stormy time they faced, and it inspired their trust as well as more open communication. And Victoria was able to recapture a leadership moment she thought she had missed.

THE WHAT HAPPENED? METHOD

Telling a story according to the What happened? method means relating the actual events that occurred as they were seen, heard, smelled, tasted, and touched. With this storytelling method, judgments, comments, opinions, and critiques are excluded, and we instead rely entirely on our powers of factual description to take our listeners on a sensory expedition through the story's landscape. An easy rule of thumb for this method would be to say what actually happened, not what you thought or felt *about* what happened. In our paradigm, this is where excavation meets crafting.

I have developed a specific framework—a creative analogy—that assists in learning and perfecting the What happened? method. It's called the What happened? camera (Figure 5.1).

According to the What happened? camera, the following are *not* facts. The camera cannot see these mental creations. While reading through the list of terms may seem obvious, you'll be surprised, when you undertake the method, how much you rely on these categories of internal experience to communicate. I would venture to say you will come to see them as crutches that you can cast away as you perfect your storytelling according to the What happened? method. Let's review:

WHAT HAPPENED? DETAILS

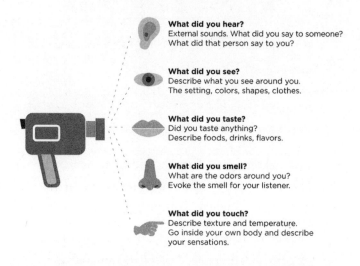

What did you hear?
External sounds. What did you say to someone?
What did that person say to you?

What did you see?
Describe what you see around you.
The setting, colors, shapes, clothes.

What did you taste?
Did you taste anything?
Describe foods, drinks, flavors.

What did you smell?
What are the odors around you?
Evoke the smell for your listener.

What did you touch?
Describe texture and temperature.
Go inside your own body and describe
your sensations.

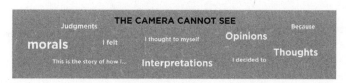

THE CAMERA CANNOT SEE

Judgments   Because

morals   I felt   I thought to myself   Opinions   Thoughts

This is the story of how I...   Interpretations   I decided to

FIGURE 5.1 **The What Happened? Camera**

Feelings: Emotions, reactions, and vague beliefs.

Interpretations: Explanations based largely on our
own version of things.

Judgments: The tendency to objectify, qualify, or
characterize someone based on our own proclivity
for certain ways of thinking or viewing others.

Opinions: Views or judgments not necessarily based on fact or knowledge; general beliefs.

Rationalizations: Attempts to justify (an action or attitude) with logical reasoning.

Commentary: The expression of opinions or offering of explanations about an event or situation.

Internal thoughts: These include comments that begin "Well, I thought to myself" or "I said to myself." These are preambles to saying what happened. When you use the What happened? camera, you don't need these preambles. So instead of saying, "I thought to myself, 'What a lovely day to take the team to lunch outside,'" you can say, "We went to the courtyard for lunch, and I said, 'Let's enjoy this lovely weather.'"

As you see, the What happened? method purposely imposes a limit. It asks you to look at your experiences fairly and squarely, stripped of meanings and judgments that all of us tend to add when telling a story. But why remove all that familiar, seemingly necessary material in order to tell a story? The answer is crucial to the success of your story and engages your listeners' natural capacity to find coherence.

When our feelings and interpretations about events are driving the show, they prevent our listeners from experiencing what happened for themselves. How can you *be there* when someone else is coloring the facts with his or her interpretation? Opinions beget opinions; judgments beget judgments. Meanwhile, when only the five sensory details are present, our audience can listen cleanly and openly. It gives space for their intelligence to assess the story's many elements.

That's the beauty of storytelling. Because we naturally project our *own* emotions and feelings onto a story we are hearing that is composed of facts, we feel immersed in a landscape, our intuition is activated, our sense of insight deepens. We react neurologically, just as we did when reading Victoria's training. It's as if we were experiencing it ourselves. That makes for a powerful experience. And it builds connection all the way through. Telling according to What happened? is the reciprocal relationship of listening and telling at its best because, in a sense, we are cocreating the story with our listeners. Of course, what we choose to tell, emphasize, and point to shapes the story arc and influences their listening. As we see where things land, how they listen and hear, we can shape our story based on that feedback.

Now let's explore the application of this method in more detail in another business situation.

DELIVERING A WOW MOMENT

A multinational medical insurance company was hit financially because of the negative reviews its customer service department was receiving online and in the media. Sparing no expense, the company brought in expert after expert in an attempt to fix the ongoing problem. Call center employees were given a set of principles that were deemed brand attributes to live by:

- Listen and learn from customers so that the customers' needs are at the heart of every decision.

- Deliver wow moments that matter.

- Always do the right thing.

- Listen to our customers.

- Be courageous and decisive.

Although the branding team patted themselves on the back for coming up with these attributes and principles, employees had no idea how to implement what amounted to a series of abstract concepts. For example, "Always do the right thing" and "Listen to our customers" are the aspirational slogans that any of the insurance company's competitors could also use.

When Narativ was brought in, we asked, "How can the company communicate its values and remedy the divide between the company and its consumers? Who has direct contact with consumers?" The answer: middle managers and call station operators.

For the company to become more consumer-centric, we saw that the entire organization needed to undergo a radical cultural change in which everyone became a storyteller. "We all need to be storytellers" became the corporate mandate. We went to the call centers and talked to the managers and reps who speak to customers every day. Our goal was to elicit their stories and share them widely to help teams be more customer-centric.

As we worked with hundreds of managers in call centers all over the world, one story in particular stuck out. Charlie, a manager, had received an escalated call, which meant that the customer had not been satisfied by any of the customer service responses she'd received so far.

This is Charlie's What happened? story:

It was a Monday night about 5:30, and I was just getting ready to leave work. I got a call from a woman named Mona.

She wanted a list of therapists for her husband, Henry.

"What kind of therapist does he need? What condition does he need to be treated for?"

Mona responded, "My husband is crazy, and he needs help. He's been diagnosed with sleep apnea, but he refuses to get the machine."

As I was talking to her, I could hear him in the background, "If you're talking to the insurance company, hang up. It's $1,200 for a machine I'm never gonna use."

I asked, "Why is he so resistant to getting a CPAP machine?"

She said she needed to go into a different room to talk.

"His father died of cancer while on a respirator. This machine looks like a respirator to him, and he's not gonna get it."

I said, "I have sleep apnea too, and I have used a CPAP machine for many years. And I'm still here."

Mona said, "You know, I really want you to talk to my husband. I want you to tell him what you're telling me."

She put him on the phone.

Henry told me that the Packers were playing the Bears and that I was taking him away from the game.

First thing I said in response was, "I'm a Bears fan."

Henry said, "Well, that's not a good start. I'm a Packers fan."

I took a breath, and I told him that Reggie White, who was an all-pro defensive player Hall of Famer, died from sleep apnea five years after retiring from professional football.

Now Henry took a breath and said, "I can't ignore this."

Oh, and by the way, his CPAP machine was covered 100 percent, so it wouldn't cost him anything.

He said he would get the machine on one condition.

"You have to say, 'Go, Pack, go!'"

I said, "You know what? If this will help you, absolutely: Go, Pack, go!"

For businesses, a What happened? story promotes the mission and goals of a company in such a way that they are graspable and memorable and powerful. When Charlie shared his story with fellow call center employees, he embodied those values and goals, and everyone immediately understood what it meant to "deliver wow moments" and "listen to our customers." They saw that they could actively create a more customer-oriented culture. Additionally, we asked people who heard stories like Charlie's to reflect on which performance characteristics they exemplified. All "brand attributes" from their circulated list naturally arose, and new ones were identified as well.

In the end, employees' stories were so well crafted and refined that they were used in an advertising campaign for the company. The result: Grateful customers. Sympathetic employees who can spread the company's message. Satisfied executives.

Now try the What happened? method. Think of the last time you were promoted or achieved a milestone at work and write down what you saw, heard, smelled, tasted, or touched. Challenge yourself not to write what you thought or felt about this moment.

Don't use more than three lines for this exercise and answer these questions to guide you:

- Were you called into someone's office to receive news of this achievement? Who was that person? What did she say to you? What did you say to her?

- Don't say what you felt or thought about the achievement—that is, don't tell us you were proud or happy. Rather, show us what pride and happiness look like for you. What happens in your body? Did you smile? Did you jump up and down? Did you call someone outside the office to tell them about the news?

- Did you celebrate the achievement or promotion? Did you go out for dinner? What did you order? Who were you with?

Notice how you feel about what you wrote. Are you engaged? Are memories of the moment that you hadn't thought of in a long time bubbling up to the surface, making new connections and associations? If so, you are experiencing the interaction that happens when we engage with this method of storytelling. Think of what's possible when you connect with your own listeners in this way and *they* feel that engagement.

If you want to see an example of absolute mastery of the What happened? approach to storytelling, look no further than Steve Jobs's commencement address at Stanford University. It has more than 9 million views on YouTube.[1]

Jobs tells the audience: "About a year ago I was diagnosed with cancer."

In that opening line, he sets the tone. He doesn't tell us what to think or feel about it; he only says what happened to him. He knows that the listener will have a feeling and thought associated to what happened to him, and he's willing to trust the listener with this line.

Here are more What happened? moments from that story:

> Later that evening I had a biopsy, where they stuck an endoscope down my throat, through my stomach, and into my intestines. Put a needle into my pancreas and got a few cells from the tumor.

Note the details. He spares us nothing. He defies all the taboos, including talking about his own body. Here's another What happened? moment:

> I was sedated, but my wife, who was there, told me that when they viewed the cells under a microscope, the doctors started crying because it turned out to be a very rare form of pancreatic cancer that is curable with surgery.

And then, with utter elegance, he simply says, "I had the surgery. I'm fine."

Notice how Jobs engages the senses in his telling, thereby igniting our imaginations. Surely, that's also part of the genius of Apple. Its products and presentations command our attention.

Now let's get back to some fine points about the method.

GOD IS IN THE DETAILS

One of the central quests of Narativ's storytelling methodology is the discovery of ways to engage the five senses and objectively tell what happened. Details derived from our sensory awareness and memory are essential. It's the details that differentiate our stories, that create context and moment.

One of the greatest difficulties with detail is choosing what to keep in and what to leave out. I have often nearly dozed off into my bowl of soup as someone at the dinner table has regaled the assembled guests with microscopic details about a work project, remodeling enterprise, or his or her problems with finding a good housekeeper. What is too much detail and too little?

Here's the thing. Detail has to serve the story. It must drive the action forward, expand our appreciation of the context, or enhance our understanding of a character. It's not there just to add some color. Detail can also intentionally slow the story down, provide a short rest stop, or accelerate the plot line. Detail has a particular function whenever it is used, similar to that of the zoom lens of the camera. It brings your listener more closely into your worldview.

To help you discover more about the power of detail, think of material objects you own and where they are placed in your home and/or office.

Quickly, without thinking too much, write down a list of five objects you own at this very moment:

1. _____

2. _____

3. _____

4. _____

5. _____

Now think of What happened? moments around each of these objects. Did someone give you the object? Did you buy it? Where is the object from? Where were you when you received it? How long have you had it? What role were you in at your work when you got this object? Who was your boss? What was happening at work at the time? What project were you working on? And then what happened?

Approach these objects with renewed curiosity, engaging your memory, and see what emerges.

One of the most memorable stories I have ever heard in a workshop was the story of a community activist whose organization was funded by one of our clients, the Open Society Foundations (George Soros's global foundation). The woman who told the story was from Zimbabwe. The training was taking place in South Africa.

I had asked that all the participants find an object that was significant to them and tell a story about it. She held up her passport and said, "This is my identity. Many people in my line of work are found dead by the side of the road, and no one knows who they were. This passport took me years to obtain, but I still went through the effort. If I die, they will find this on me and know who I was. This is my identity."

DIALOGUE

Dialogue is an extraordinarily powerful and efficient way to capture significant turning points and to advance character and action. In fact, it will probably be one of the main ways you solve what is at first considered to be the biggest challenge of the What happened? method: How do I talk about what I was thinking or someone else was feeling? People say what they think or feel. You and your characters can too.

Take these words:

"Don't go."

Just two words. And you've got the beginning of a story that immediately captures our attention. In just two words, you've set up at least two characters and two powerful actions in an extraordinarily economical way. Action 1:

Someone is going. Action 2: Someone else is trying to stop him or her.

In adhering to the rule of telling only what happened, Narativ's storytelling methodology bears a close resemblance to the art of the screenwriter who is enjoined to *show* rather than *tell*, using the visual medium of film. In screenwriting, dialogue is a crucial medium for revealing character.

Like the screenwriter, we cannot resort to *character-izations*. For example, "He was *generous*," "She was *evil*," "He *lacked courage*." These descriptions are interpretations. They tell rather than show.

Dialogue not only reveals character but also serves the following functions:

- It moves the story forward.

- It communicates facts and information to the audience.

- It establishes relationships.

- It reveals conflict and power dynamics.

- It expresses the emotional states of characters.

It is also important to remember that what people do *not* say (omissions) can be just as powerful as what they do. For example, you might say, "That Sunday morning, I didn't go to the park. I drove to the office and swiped my keycard at the entrance, where one of the five security guards was on duty." Saying that you didn't go to the park on a Sunday and instead went to the office creates a whole other perspective on what happened. What didn't happen is just as powerful as what did happen!

WHAT ABOUT EMOTION?

Whenever I teach Narativ's Listening and Storytelling Method, these questions recur: "If you stick only to what happened, how do you convey emotions?" "What good is a story without emotions?" The questions are based on at least two faulty premises. First, that addressing What happened? excludes the possibility of conveying emotions and, second, that telling about emotions actually *communicates* them.

Our brain mirrors information we receive about the five senses, so there's less need to be told interpretive information; we automatically fill in the gaps with our own experience. When "Bob walked into the room, slammed the door, and looked out the window, away from me," my listeners don't need more cues to imagine emotions of anger or pain or frustration. As the story proceeds, the delicate choices I make in What happened? moments will continue to fill in the picture. Our audience brings with them all the emotions a story will ever need. We can enjoy choosing details that activate and engage those emotions for dramatic effect and to highlight the message of our story.

A great example of leaving out emotions from the telling of the story and sticking only to what happened came through our work with a multinational pharmaceutical company. The company leaders asked Narativ to support their efforts to foster cross-communication among the research and sales teams and to present their findings in ways that were not so driven by dry and raw data, which they found was falling flat with audiences everywhere, both internal and external. They wanted to find ways for researchers to explain their work through personal stories that could, in turn, be incorporated into sales strategies.

Stella was on the clinical research team, working on treatments for Alzheimer's. Her Why story? question was answered by the company. They had chosen storytelling as the most effective form of communication. But Why now? Stella's answer to this question was deeply personal, having to do with her relationship with her father.

She told the following story using the What happened? method. This was her story after all interpretations, commentaries, and judgments were stripped away:

My father was a doctor back in Shanghai, where I was born. He combined Western and traditional

Chinese medicine, inventing new methods for treating scleroderma. Patients from all over the world came to see him. Whether we were at home eating dinner or he was relaxing in an armchair listening to the radio on the weekend, people would knock on our door and say, "My child has a high fever" or "My mother is ill. What should I do?"

My father immediately jumped on his bicycle and raced to see them. Since he refused to take money from them, people would give us eggs or knit him a hat.

At the age of 70 my father had a stroke, which developed into Alzheimer's.

To this day, whenever I visit Shanghai, his old patients run up to me in the streets, and they tell me how much they miss him.

If he'd had the medicines Stella was developing in the laboratory, he'd probably be alive and working today.

For Stella, it was unusual to talk about her personal life at work. But her father had just passed away. In fact, both her parents passed away within three months of each other, and that was a difficult period for her. Even though she had described herself as a very private person, she felt very emotional telling her story.

She expressed emotions in a form that allowed her to publicly honor and pay tribute to her father. As the story revealed how her work was tightly connected to her memory of her father, the impact on her audience was complete engagement. They were ready to hear what insights her research had gained into the products the sales team was going to sell. Without that emotional atmosphere, her presentation would not have landed in such a memorable way.

Interestingly, because stories and emotions are so inseparably interwoven, when we provide a corporate training, we almost invariably meet with the question, "What is the role of emotion in the workplace?" There is almost a circular logic at work here: we can't really imagine a story without emotion, yet storytelling in business provokes the question about emotion's role and place at work. But isn't the workplace one of the stories of our lives? Won't it naturally evoke emotional experiences?

Indeed, things that happen to us at work flood us with emotions. The point is that thinking critically when ruled by emotions becomes a nearly impossible task. We need first to acknowledge that emotions are a powerful force, whether at work or at home, that they carry powerful potential to affect communication (for better or worse), and that we need a way to integrate them successfully. Let's look at how the What happened? method speaks directly to this communication conundrum.

If we're upset about a coworker's comment, or our own performance, or perhaps the challenge posed by a client, we may succumb to a prevalent cultural dichotomy in America and set aside our emotions (at best) or suppress them forcefully (at worst) as we grapple with communicating about these events. Here, the discipline of the What happened? method allows us to recall those experiences without rejecting our emotions by simply putting the facts first. This creates space for some discrimination to enter our reflection on our experience. "Hmm, what happened there outside of my reaction to it? Let me recollect that event." Try this for yourself right now. Tell yourself a What happened? story about something emotionally charged or about which you have lots of opinions and judgments. Be disciplined. Just the facts.

One version of your story might go as follows. "Xander always comes late to meetings because he just doesn't care about the project or the team, and he's probably consumed with just his own career path forward—let's not mention the sloppy way he keeps his office!" Why not rewind and recount these observations from a What happened? perspective. "Xander came to the meeting after everyone else. In fact, the meeting had already started. Earlier, when I entered his office, I saw piles of paper on his desk and on the floor. His computer screen displayed websites unrelated to our work." Okay, still, possibly a damning set of facts. But you see the difference, right? There's space, almost a coolness, to telling or reading a factual account.

That space is a precious asset for all of us, but it is especially so in business, where we are being asked to bring the best of our *critical intelligence* to work. "Professional" is supposed to mean that we put aside biases, judgments, opinions, and other prejudices and analyze things with some objectivity. The What happened? method is a tool that assists us in doing exactly that.

Following this method takes a tremendous amount of discipline. The tendency to slip into interpretation and then judgment is almost as automatic as breathing. But note that you can parse the emotional content of a situation using the What happened? method *only if you've identified and released the obstacles to listening.* An emotional overlay becomes obvious to us as an obstacle to listening and telling the moment we begin to use the What happened? method. We'll find ourselves needing to prune one interpretation or opinion after the next. The more we adhere to it, the more we can remove these obstacles to our communication. By saying what happened and detailing the facts of your experience, you can bring yourself and others into a clearer picture of events without clouding their listening with the language of emotions.

This brings our communication forward, allowing emotions their place but not allowing them to tangle up what we want to say. Notice the distinction we are making here: we allow the emotions to come up; we identify them; but then we release them and don't allow them to direct us.

This is why we follow What happened? like our North Star in storytelling and as a principle in our communication.

KEY POINTS TO REMEMBER

1. Tell what happened according to the five senses. If you can't hear it, taste it, smell it, touch it, and/or see it, then it didn't happen.

2. Take out all interpretations, opinions, judgments, statements of feeling, and anything else that the What happened? camera would not be able to see.

3. No morals or lessons learned. Those do not belong in the story. Let your listeners be free to make up their own moral or lesson.

4. Trust your listeners' ability to understand your message, thanks to your description of what happened to you.

5. This method takes discipline and practice. Keep at it. It will pay off.

6. The goal of your story is to connect with your listeners. Saying what happened allows for that connection to happen. If your listeners have questions or want to start a dialogue or even tell their own story after you've said what happened to you, then you know you've connected.

WHEN TO USE THE WHAT HAPPENED? CAMERA

1. Every time you've determined that a story is the most appropriate way to communicate your message, then your story should answer the question "What happened?"

2. If you are in a meeting, whether in a group or one-on-one, where emotions are running high because someone is upset about something (or you are), ask What happened? to cut through the fog of emotions and get to the heart of the matter. The details you bring up by asking What happened? can be acted on as a source of solutions to situations that you may have found challenging to deal with in the past.

3. When you find yourself stuck in front of a blank page or don't know where to go next in a

conversation with someone, say what happened next. Think about the actions you took, what was said to you, what you said to others, and you will move forward.

Remember that this method takes practice. Lots of practice. Please do not be discouraged at the outset when our habits of relating experience through a complex mixture of interpretation, opinion, and judgment get in the way. Slow down and enjoy reflecting on the details of what happened. It can be refreshing. And revealing. For sure, you will only get better by trying it out with others. See how your stories land with others when you tell what happened.

Receive their listening and see how it impacts your listeners when you tell them your story in this way.

Here are a few more scenarios in which What happened? can help move the needle toward your goals.

Leadership

A company changes management, going from two leaders to one and a restructuring period that leads to layoffs of 30 percent of the staff. A leader can use What happened? to tell the story of the breakup and rationale for change, being specific about what is changing and what impact it will have on the company.

Telling what happened is about facing facts and not straying from them, which is critical when navigating change.

Sales

Use What happened? as a way to move away from the dryness of the features of the products you're selling. Customers can find all that in the product manual. Instead, describe what the products do for people. Tell what happened when the product is in someone's home or office.

Team Collaboration

When we worked with the design group of a large tech company, we gathered teams of engineers, product managers, and designers together to create What happened? stories that transformed ideas into pitch presentations. The teams were not accustomed to collaborating on presenting to the COO and CEO their latest ideas. Instead, they were used to working on building a prototype for months, working individually, and coming together only a few days before pitching. The new head of the design group felt this was wasteful and that there should be a way to present ideas early without having to build a version of the product.

Enter What happened? stories. These stories mixed use cases with motivation and inspiration to showcase new ideas by grounding them in concrete experiences.

Onboarding

We were approached by a CEO who had just been funded for a year to develop her burgeoning idea. In other words, she was a one-woman show. She began by excavating and crafting her origin story to inspire funders and partners to follow her. As her team grew, she kept engaging us to work on her evolving story. And then her team reached a point where she wanted everyone to be able to tell their origin story about why this business mattered to them, so that she would not be the only one with a powerful and engaging story about the business.

The What happened? stories her team developed became onboarding tools for newcomers, inspiring them to come up with their own stories but also, and most critically, to prepare them for their jobs, saving them precious time training on the job. Using the What happened? method, they continued to create collections of "knowledge stories" by telling and collecting What happened? stories about people's jobs, describing specifically what everyone does and making it graspable for any newcomer. This meant that newcomers didn't have to rely on outdated training videos and dry, impersonal standard operating manuals.

WHAT HAPPENED? EXERCISES

Now it's your turn. Take some time to go through the following two exercises. These will help you excavate What happened? moments.

The 10 Incidents Exercise

This is an exercise that is best done when you have identified and released your obstacles to listening, especially self-judgment or self-critical thoughts and feelings.

Once you have released your obstacles to listening, *quickly*—without thinking too much about it and without any self-judgment—make a list of 10 incidents in your life that could be elaborated into stories. This may come to you as a title (for example, "The CEO Pitch Meeting"); an event (for example, "The Day I Quit"); a place (for example, "Entering My Grandpa's Shop"); or a person (for example, "Jenny's First Marathon"):

1. _____

2. _____

3. _____

4. _____

5. _____

6. _____

7. _____

8. _____

9. _____

10. _____

We do this to get our creative juices flowing, so that we see there are possibilities for stories in many different types of life events, big and small.

What Happened? Sentences Exercise

Below are examples of sentences and how they can be changed into What happened? statements.

"I tried not to show that I was angry. But I was so pissed off."

"Angry" is a description of a feeling. According to What happened?, you might say: "My hands were shaking. I clenched my jaw. I didn't say anything after he cut me off and told me, 'That's a stupid idea.'"

That is a story describing what happened. There are clearly feelings going on here, but they are not named.

"I worked for an abusive manager."

The word "abusive" is an interpretation. Here's the What happened? translation of that interpretation: "My manager threw a book at me. I ducked, and it hit the wall."

"I don't like the way this client addresses me. It's disrespectful."

The What happened? camera cannot see "disrespectful" or not liking the way someone does or says something. Here's what the What happened? camera can see: "I walked into the boardroom, and the client didn't look at me. He gestured toward the chair and said one word: sit."

"I don't think the middle America market is going to like this product."

That statement has no fact associated with it and doesn't pass the What happened? camera test. The following sentence does: "Our market study shows

that 55 percent of people living in Idaho would pur-
chase our new line of cleaning products."

"I decided to call my counterpart in China and ask
about a situation I was dealing with."

Deciding to do something is not an action you can
see, hear, touch, taste, or smell. Similarly, explaining
an action you took without telling us about the action
itself results in a statement that doesn't show us action or point toward resolution. However, the camera
can record this: "I picked up the phone and dialed
Jiang's phone number in Shenzhen. I told him we
needed to talk about the latest shipment that never
arrived. He said he would talk to his supervisor and
call me back."

"Our team desperately needs equipment."

How can this supervisor use the What happened?
method to support his request for more computers?
He might say: "We haven't bought the three computers for the new hires that we promised we would
get as part of our budget. Last month, Gary brought
his laptop, Michelle worked from home, and Justine
shared a desktop with her supervisor. They are all
asking for their own computers."

Now take a look at the examples that follow. Some are What happened? sentences, while others are not. Find the sentences that are not and transform them by using the What happened? camera just as we did with the previous examples:

- I overheard her say the most horrible thing. It made me so angry.

- It was cold outside. My body was shivering, and my teeth were chattering.

- I opened the window and screamed.

- I thought, "There is no way I'm calling him."

- I crossed the finish line sweating and crying.

- I felt so alone.

- I didn't look into his eyes when I said, "I think it's over."

- I decided to get on the plane and find her.

- My father came home in a new white Mercedes.

- I remember the way my mother's cooking smelled.

- His explanation was long and boring.

- I heard a dog barking across the street.

- That day I learned that I could accomplish anything.

- She said to me, "I always knew you could accomplish anything."

- I said, "It doesn't matter to me anymore" because I was so done with it all.

- I realized in that moment that it was never my fault.

How did you do? Deceptively simple, right? Remember that this is a discipline and that you get better as you practice. So keep practicing.

A MENTAL DISCIPLINE

The What happened? method is how we *craft* our story. We do it moment by moment, event by event, slowly but surely. Have confidence that you are building a powerful story. The user manual for this communication tool is your own willingness to work through its unfamiliarity until you become handy with it. Let your creativity flourish. Experiment and enjoy. You'll be amazed at the precision you develop and the dimensions you begin to see around any event, object, or person.

In the long run, What happened? becomes a kind of mental discipline. It reminds us to keep things simple and to the point, to stick to the facts. So many participants in our workshops tell us how much more focused and directed they've become as presenters or in their speech in general as a result of practicing this method. More than anything else, it familiarizes us with our tendency toward judgment, opinion, and commentary. We might be surprised to notice that when relating an event, say, or how one coworker behaves, we are often talking entirely from opinion and judgment! Gently returning to What happened? allows us to see things clearly again. The more we do, the more our greater intelligence comes through. Who doesn't benefit from that perspective? You and your audience certainly will.

6

FIND YOUR
ENDING

n this chapter, we'll look at story arc, the traditional passage from beginning to end, with a middle that contains an emotional turning point. This is where you put all the pieces and principles together. Here are the steps so far: You've excavated a story from life experiences, which began with answering the potent questions, Why story? Why now? You've envisioned your audience, followed by identifying and releasing any obstacles to your listening. You've experienced the catalytic effect of the Grandparent Exercise, and your storytelling muscles have been stretched. Finally, you've gathered your story's parts through the What happened? method. Now you craft the story in earnest.

In this book, we've delineated steps and lessons. In practice, the dynamic, reciprocal process of listening and telling through which you produce a story is not always linear. Excavation can quickly lead to crafting; in crafting, you may discover more excavation is necessary. After presenting, you may see things in a new light. Excavating, crafting, and presenting are equal components of a live process of discovery. Fluidity and responsiveness to new insights come with time.

DEVELOPING CRAIG'S STORY

Although it's difficult to describe the process in a nonlinear way, walking you through my coaching of Craig Kostelic, chief business officer of the Food Innovation Group (FIG) at Condé Nast, will expose the real nuts and bolts of story creation. It will also starkly contrast the power of business storytelling in a personal way with other modes of communication.

As you've read in Chapter 1, Craig has a richly formulated answer to the question, Why story? Why now? He recognizes that excellence in storytelling is fundamental to his team's success. Now he wants to create his own personal narrative that will communicate his belief, passion, and values to his team. He wants a story that expresses how he views himself as a leader and his coworkers as a team. Ultimately, he wants his company to excel, and he believes that every story counts.

In this first iteration of his presentation, before working with Narativ, Craig had prepared a speech and delivered it to his team members at the Food Innovation Group during their summit. A day was being devoted to a new initiative titled "As It's Told: The Story and the Sell."

Craig, a 32-year-old former high school and college football player, wore a finely tailored suit and stood at the podium in front of the room. As text flowed onscreen à la *Star Wars*, he shared this tongue-in-cheek narrative, with appreciation and inspiration as his goal:

> We are a company with some of the most iconic brands in the world. As technology changed the way the world was consuming content, this innovative group knew that things needed to be done differently. They needed to change the way that the publishing side interacts with the editorial side. They needed less bureaucracy. They needed to reinvent what it meant to collaborate and cocreate with advertisers.
>
> This innovative group proved to be wise beyond their years. As when the iconic company they were a part of was figuring out how to adapt to this new world, this innovative group enjoyed unparalleled success. It was at that moment that the iconic company's leaders knew they needed a seismic change to replicate the power of this innovative group. As much as a seismic change was

needed at the iconic company as a whole, this change threatened the very way of life for this innovative group. Undeterred in the face of possible extinction, this innovative group, through their willpower, determination, and a culture they had built, defied all odds, broke free, remained independent, and continued their quest for food media domination.

When I began to coach Craig in developing a personal What happened? leadership story, we analyzed this presentation. Although his speech captured key points in the change story of his group, he saw how generic it was and how it could apply to anything or anyone. It was forgettable. He wanted to find a way to make his message more personal and more potent. He wanted a signature *origin story* to demonstrate who he is, where he comes from, and how he sees the world. He wanted to convey his distinct leadership qualities and how they would continue to bolster the success of everybody on the team. He would be there for them. And he wanted to show them how.

When I'm working with a client one-on-one, I take the role of a dedicated listener and devote my attention to the client's story. For the storyteller, this kind of listening is both encouraging and liberating. With the feeling that your story is being genuinely listened to, you find yourself telling it in a new way, as the listener's full attention creates a container for your creativity to fill.

As a leader, Craig has a naturally strong relationship with storytelling. "I've always appreciated the power of words and the power of stories," he told us. "My personal drive was in a sense captured in the story I was telling myself as I climbed the ladder to success," he continued. It was a way of encouraging himself to persevere and deal with different obstacles that were in his way. Craig's position in the company quickly grew. From where he sits now, he sees a new role for story in his leadership, one closely tied to his understanding of team dynamics.

"Rather than figuring out how *I* take the next step up the ladder, for me now, I see it's all about the success of the group." Craig realized that there had to be "a bigger purpose" to pull everyone onto the same page and connect them so that they worked as a cohesive whole. He intuitively knew that a story would express that more than numbers would. As we talked, Craig related his experiences as a football player in high school and college. What emerged was a set of experiences that were formative for his character. These experiences were in fact where much of his self-definition originated:

Playing sports growing up and having different coaches and a lot of different teammates, you are put in some situations that can be uncomfortable for you. This made an impact on how "leaned in" you were and how much you cared and how much you were willing to sacrifice—or not—for the greater good of the team.

For me, the most important thing as I lead an organization is making sure that the culture is a place that people want to come to every day and that they feel supported; that they actually like each other and care about one another and want what's best for one another; and that they know, as I'm playing the role of head coach, that I give a shit about their personal development. I care about having an open-door policy and making sure that their needs are met both personally and professionally. I want them to have opportunity and a voice.

The parallels Craig was drawing between his early experiences in team sports and his role as "head coach" of his "team" at work were uncanny in their relevance. But we didn't want to simply "tell" the lessons and inspirations he drew from those experiences. We wanted to "show" them so that they could function with unmodified power, the power only storytelling can deliver.

STORY STRUCTURE: BEGINNING, EMOTIONAL TURNING POINT, AND ENDING

The success of a story depends largely on its structure. Through the What happened? method, you plot out the details. At that point, your story is simply a succession of What happened? moments. To become a satisfying story, those moments will have to be shaped into three parts: beginning, emotional turning point, and ending.

Story Arc and Turning Points

Every story has an arc. Telling a story can be likened to being the pilot of a passenger plane. You are taking your audience on a journey. The beginning of the story is like the takeoff. Just as the pilot has the engines at full throttle for takeoff, so does the storyteller have a relatively short time to actively engage the attention of the audience.

Ending a story can be compared to landing the plane. Like the pilot who must know how to descend, precisely where to land and come to a full standstill, the story-teller must guide the audience toward the conclusion, and bring the story to a significant end. In between is the flight itself, and though no one likes turbulence, a bumpy ride does make for a better story. Just so, your story will be more captivating when you've identified your emotional turning point (Figure 6.1).

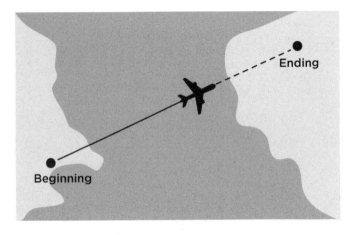

FIGURE 6.1 **Flight Analogy**

Where to Begin

If the very first sentence (or two) of your story captures our attention, then we, your listeners, will follow you wherever your story takes us. Take the lead, know where you're going, and we'll go with you. In fact, we'll *want* to go with you. A strong beginning is always a What happened? beginning. With your first line you can choose to drop us right in the middle of the action. Being dropped into the middle of a story sparks our curiosity because we are not given a context. We do not know quite what is going on, and the mystery of it makes us want to know what happens next. *Example:* "My wife turned around and picked up the phone. 'It's for you. She says she's a headhunter.'"

Your beginning can be starkly simple. This approach is the opposite of drawing a detailed picture, and it can be just as dramatic. Start your story with a short sentence (or two) that demands attention. It can be shocking, hilarious, improbable—anything, as long as it's simple and riveting. *Example:* "I walked into the room where my boss and the HR director were sitting at the conference table. Ten minutes later I was walking out the revolving doors of the building with a box of my personal photos and the pencil holder my wife had given me."

When you're new to storytelling, the Narativ rule of thumb for where to start your story is: *Start somewhere.* Just start. If you need to add or subtract context, that's easy enough to do later. Don't judge yourself or spin your wheels. Over time, you'll develop a keener sense of the relationship between where you start and where you end. Your beginnings will become less random and begin to function as subtle ways of setting up the ending, the punch line. That relationship is why this chapter is titled "Find Your Ending." But we'll get into that more a bit later.

As I worked with Craig, you'll see how we crafted a beginning that from the get-go would point toward an impactful ending. In a four-minute story, you have to be aiming at your ending. Initially, Craig shared a story he had told in his weekly sales meeting:

> Every Wednesday evening, we have our weekly sales meeting with the entire team, and we get together for 60 to 90 minutes. At the last meeting, I told a story about different environments or the different situations in which I had played high school football and the connection I felt to my team and the connection I felt to my coach.
>
> What that did, coupled with my passion, was, it gave me willingness to sacrifice for the greater good of the team in a way that I didn't even need to think about twice. And contrasting that with the situation I had in college, where the connection to the entire group of teammates wasn't as strong as it had been to the high school team and the connection with the coach wasn't nearly as strong. So when I was asked to sacrifice or push myself in an unnatural position, it gave me an excuse to put my hands up and quit.
>
> And again, looking at those two situations 10 to 15 years later, I think it's clear to me that the connection to the group and to the leader were the two biggest variables in terms of how I felt about sacrifice or pushing myself in an unnatural position.

The immediate problem with this story is that it doesn't tell What happened? It contains self-characterization—that is, it describes what kind of person Craig is—but little action. We might describe it as an "internal narrative," a story we tell ourselves, which is our everyday mode of story, a kind of dialogue with ourselves we use to make sense of and retain elements of experiences for processing. In storytelling, we want to strip all that out. You've got to start with an action, something that can be seen, heard, touched, tasted, or smelled. I asked Craig, "What was a specific thing that happened that demonstrated the quality of your different coaches?" In other words, was there something that happened on the team, something dramatic or emotional that would form the core of the story?

He responded:

So you have freshman football, and you go become a sophomore, and that's when you're on the varsity team. When I became a sophomore, the coach who had been there for a while and had had a lot of success retired, and the school board made a decision to go with an outsider instead of one of his assistant coaches, who would have continued operating as things had been operating—which is what most people wanted. But they made the decision to go with an outsider. He came in during my sophomore year. He had a so-so year with a lot of issues, and my junior year they ended up letting him go and hiring a person who was more part of that prior system.

Here again Craig was explaining a situation in a vague and abstract way. The audience would need something more to hold on to. I asked Craig to show me something about his relationship to football. What would I have seen? This is excavation at work: We've identified a general area for the collection of a story, but we're not hot yet; we're still following the scent of a better story. My storytelling antennae perked up when Craig began to tell me about his family watching football on TV:

If you ever came to my house on a Sunday morning or early afternoon, you would see 10 people huddled around the TV, watching the Steelers.

And there you have it. A What happened? beginning. It drops us right into the middle of the scene, which shows (rather than tells) where Craig's from. The setting is an intimate yet animated family scene. As the listener, I am hooked, and my brain activates my own memories of being with my family around the TV. I identify with the teller and want to find out what happens next.

We spent more time excavating. I asked him questions to help trigger his senses. I was looking for something specific that had happened that would advance action and develop character.

We uncovered a moment when Craig told his parents he wanted to be a football player. I pushed for details and listened. He related a newfound memory, explaining that before football, he had played soccer. His mother didn't want him to play football due to the danger of concussions. His father felt differently. Every story requires some kind of conflict, and here we have a disagreement. As I pushed harder for details, we landed upon two events with which Craig now begins his origin story:

> I'm seven years old, sitting in my bedroom with my ear against the door so I can eavesdrop on the conversation my parents are having in the kitchen. "It's not a safe sport, Chuck. He could get hurt," my mother says.
>
> "We have to let him try things out and explore. He'll be fine," my father responds.
>
> Growing up, every Sunday afternoon in the fall meant the entire family huddled around the TV draped in black and gold from head to toe. My mother, Paulette, is fussing around in the kitchen with Aunt Chic, ordering pizza and making her

famous buffalo chicken dip. My father, Chuck, is fixing a beer and a shot for Uncle Joe while telling him, "You know, I think this year is our year."

The Emotional Turning Point

In traditional dramatic structure, a conflict or obstacle arises that the main character somehow has to overcome or resolve. It's what everyone's silently anticipating when you begin a story, and it will be the surefire way to make your message or meaning stick. Imagine a story without one: "I went to the store and bought bread before walking home." "Mr. Bradley told the client about the new software update and finished the call." Something's missing, right?

Our brains are hardwired to create and respond to storytelling structure. However, the choices we make about where to start and end and what turning points to include rely in part on creative inspiration but also on a solid and practiced understanding of dramatic action. What makes a story really work? What makes us, the audience, move to the edge of our seats?

Did you reach your goal or destination, or didn't you? What are the obstacles you encountered along the way? It's a well-worn cliché that all drama needs conflict. What the cliché lacks is subtlety. *Conflict* connotes your struggle to achieve your goal. It can just as easily be funny,

touching, moving, or violent. Remember, we want to
see transformation in your story. Something changes;
you as the lead character transforms, even if it is a subtle change. Conflict is inherently dramatic. It creates sus-
pense and tension, pulling your listeners into your story
so that they identify with you in wanting to resolve the
conflict or overcome the obstacle. When structuring your
story, moments of conflict are turning points—the places
where the story changes direction (Figure 6.2).

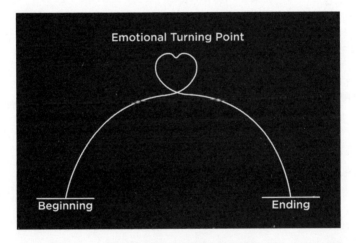

FIGURE 6.2 **Emotional Turning Point**

When you look back over your life, you can identify the highest and lowest emotional points, the moments that changed where your life was headed. Maybe
it was the birth of a child, an argument you had with
your mother, a chance meeting with one of your heroes,
or a failure or a promotion.

Craig's Emotional Turning Point

Having established the importance of football in his life, we continued to excavate and craft Craig's story in the dialogic process of our method, which led to the discovery of his point of highest emotion: "After the game, while my teammates celebrated our first victory, I took off my pads and was the first one out of the locker room. I went home and got in the shower, sat on the floor, and cried. The rest of the season went by without me seeing the field again."

Notice that this is rendered entirely in the What happened? method and how much emotion it delivers. Now that Craig has his beginning and he has discovered his emotional turning point, it's time to head directly to his ending.

Ending

After we discovered the emotional turning point, I continued to coach Craig to find his end. Since he had told me about the support of his father, which became a part of his beginning, I asked him if he had had any conversations with him during the emotional point.

Craig recalled, "Here's one thing my father said when I told him I didn't want to be in this school district anymore and that I wanted us to move: 'We are absolutely not moving. You need to accept your failures and learn from them.'"

I reminded him how powerful a little bit of dialogue can be to point to a bad feeling or express that you are questioning your confidence or your ability, which are internal and can't be seen by the What happened? camera.

This memory would become pivotal as a transition from the turning point to the end, but we weren't there yet. With a bit more excavation, Craig revealed that in the season's last game, his team faced an opponent they hadn't beaten in 10 years. The Aliquippa Quips were ranked number 1 in the state. And they defeated the Quips 12 nothing!

Craig took some time to map out the entire story and get it back to me. I'd like to share the story that Craig excavated and crafted with me from beginning to end:

I'm seven years old, sitting in my bedroom with my ear against the door so I can eavesdrop on the conversation my parents are having in the kitchen. "It's not a safe sport, Chuck. He could get hurt," my mother says.

"We have to let him try things out and explore, Paul. He'll be fine," my father says.

Growing up, every Sunday afternoon in the fall, the entire family huddled around the TV draped in black and gold from head to toe. My mother, Paulette, is in the kitchen with Aunt Chic, ordering pizza and making her famous buffalo chicken dip. My father, Chuck, is fixing a shot and a beer for Uncle Joe while telling him, "You know, I think this year is our year."

It's midsummer 1999, and I am on my back deck. "You won't be the captain. You probably won't even play that much," my dad tells me.

"Playing with the older kids will force me to play against bigger and faster competition, and it will get me used to the speed of the game for high school," I tell my father.

"I think you're making the right decision, but it won't be easy," my father says as he finishes his glass of red wine and gives me a strong pat on the back.

The first scrimmage in junior high was on a hot summer afternoon in late August against the Elwood City Wolverines. Our locker room was a mile from the field where the scrimmages took place. I put on my helmet and snapped my chin-strap on while the team got in a two-by-two formation. The metal spikes on our shoes clanked on the pavement in unison as we made our way to Sarge Alberts Field.

Thirty minutes into the scrimmage, "Second team defense out!" Coach Beatrice yelled as I sprinted onto the field. As the offense broke the huddle and lined up in formation, I started pumping my knees to my chest, like I'd seen Jack Lambert do in the old Pittsburgh Steelers tapes I used to watch with my father. "Down, set, hut!" the quarterback screamed as he took the ball from the center and handed it to the running back. There were "ohhs" from the people in the stands as I drove the crown of my helmet into the facemask of the ball carrier the moment he got the ball. "Number 10 showed up to play today!" Coach Beatrice screamed from the sidelines as my teammates pulled me off the ground and slapped me on the helmet.

Two years later, "Starting at middle linebacker for the Center Trojans, sophomore Craig Kostelic," I heard from the loud speaker as I ran onto the field for my first varsity game under the Friday night lights.

We lost that game to the Mohawk Indians 49 to 7.

Three days later, the team gathered on the practice field. "The tape doesn't lie," Coach Savage said. "Effort and discipline take zero talent. Look in the mirror and ask yourself if you played all four quarters on Friday night. I want players who give it everything they've got every second they are on the field."

Five days later, I watched from the sidelines while my team beat the Freedom Bulldogs 20 to 7.

After the game, while my teammates celebrated our first victory, I took off my pads and was the first one out of the locker room. I went home and got in the shower, sat on the floor, and cried.

The rest of the season went by without me seeing the field again.

"Coach Savage is a piece of shit. To hell with him. He's jealous and resentful that he was never good enough. I want to move school districts," I said to my father.

"You want me to move our family because you weren't good enough to stay on the field?" my father shot back at me. "Son, you have some physical talent, but you aren't mentally strong. One thing didn't go your way, and you shut down on your coaches and teammates. You took the easy way out. Most people run away from failure; they want to deny its existence. If you want to be successful, not just in football but in life, embrace your failure. Own it. Understand it. Learn from it. Let it be the reason you wake up for workouts earlier than anyone else, why you're the last one on the practice field every single day.

Failure—when used properly—is the single greatest gift you can ever ask for."

"Blessed Is He Who Accepts Failure Without Despair" is a tattoo in cursive over my heart. I had that done after finishing my high school career and accepting a scholarship to play linebacker at Bucknell University.

That's Craig's ending. When he went back to look at his entire map of the story, he took out the part about defeating the school's football rival, he fleshed out what his father had told him, and he excavated the quote that is featured on his tattoo.

It leaves a mark, doesn't it? Figuratively and literally. Imagine the effect of this quote on his team. He will capture their imagination, and any message he needs to deliver to them will undoubtedly be remembered.

As you can see from Craig's story, as you are excavating and crafting your story, the ending may not be immediately clear. That's okay. Although sometimes you are dead sure of where you want to end, in most cases, the ending emerges from the story creation process. The important thing to keep in mind is that you are seeking an experience in which the emotions of your conflict are released. That will give you an ending that delivers, that lands, and that recapitulates the rationale for your story in one short moment.

Craig experienced failure and found resolution in his father's sage advice. The story shows this life lesson or moral. It doesn't tell it, lecture, or advise.

You may be tempted to reiterate the lesson captured in your story. Don't. It will be that much more powerful if you leave it to the audience to come to their own conclusions and draw meaning from the origin story you tell.

After we concluded the coaching session that led to his ending, Craig wrote to me, "Finding the end gave me the confidence to tell my story." When we speak about finding your ending, we are bridging the gap between crafting and presenting. In crafting, your ending is a landmark, a place to get to, a necessary tension with your beginning. Once you've crafted it, knowing your ending is your confidence. It's your way of holding your audience's attention even before you've begun. We'll look at that more in the next chapter.

Your Origin Story Exercise

Using Craig's story as inspiration, develop your own origin story. Think of the major emotional turning points in your life that led you to where you are today. Make a list of those moments in just a few sentences. You could write down something that was said to you or something you said to someone else.

Now that you've identified these moments, choose one and create a story map that has a beginning and an end:

First line: _____

_____

Last line: _____

_____

Emotional turning point 1 (point of highest emotion in the story): _____

_____

Now that you have your first and last lines and your emotional turning point, place them along your story arc. This will form the basis of your story presentation.

You've used the prompt Why story? Why now? to uncover your rationale for telling a story. You have excavated a story according to the What happened? method and laid those moments out along a story arc. Now you have everything you need to present your story.

7

CONNECT WITH YOUR AUDIENCE

From the moment you ask the questions Why story? Why now?, you have begun thinking about your relationship with an audience. Every subsequent step in Narativ's method is oriented toward optimizing your creation of a connection with your audience. Connection is your Lion's Gaze.

Having excavated your story and crafted a beginning, emotional turning point, and end, you are ready to present. The best way to learn how to present is to do it. Offer people your story. Then ask them if they are willing to listen. If the answer is yes, then you are bound into a listening and storytelling contract. Try this with more than one person, maybe your family or your team at work. At all times remember the reciprocal relationship of listening and telling. What follows are guidelines and principles for presentation.

CONNECT TO YOUR BODY

A story lives in your body. Your body remembers your story, and therefore your body is an instrument of telling. As part of your preparation for telling, it's important to search your body for tension that may interfere. The best place to scan the body for obstacles is in the actual physical space where the story is going to be told.

Imagine the experience of an actor who walks onto the empty stage where she will perform. Immediately she will have an audience within her listening, and that usually begins to influence how she will feel about her body and the story contained within it. Performers have many exercises to prepare the body for presentation. If you can, go to the space where you will tell your story and engage in the following exercise drawn from the Alexander technique, which teaches that there needs to be a relaxed relationship between head, neck, and spine, achieved by undoing habitual reactions and tensions.

Find a place to lie flat on your back, with enough space around you so that you're not touching anything. Relax your neck by resting your head on a small pile of books. Draw up your legs. Relaxing your shoulder joints and elbows, place your hands on your rib cage, one at a time. Now direct your body to become heavy and to release into the ground beneath you. Keeping your eyes open (so you don't fall asleep), make a mental note of any tensions in your body, loosening them by being aware especially of your out breath. Allow yourself to release your spine farther and farther into the ground, which naturally elongates the relationship between the top of your head and your sit bones. You will experience an overall settling of the body into a more natural balance. When you rise, roll over on your side, and then pressing hands and feet into the floor, slowly come to standing while releasing all tension in your neck.

If the presentation space is not available and you have your own private office, practice there, or find a private space elsewhere, such as a conference room. For maximum effectiveness, practice the technique at home, lying down for 15 minutes at a time. That way, after even a few minutes of lying down at work, your body will remember the relaxation response. The more grounded you become in this way, the more power your presentation will draw from your body as the storehouse for your story. This technique clears not only bodily tension but also tension that restricts optimal vocal production. The voice is an instrument of your telling as well, and having maximum range from soft to loud is important.

CONNECT TO THE SPACE

In presentation, you are always working with *proprioception*, which is defined as the instinctive perception of the position and movements of the body.

To begin, think about the space in which you might tell your story. Imagine Craig Kostelic telling his story at Condé Nast's offices on the thirty-fourth floor of the new World Trade Center. Think about the history of that building and all that it signifies across the world. Picture sweeping views of the Statue of Liberty, the Hudson River, the skyscrapers and the bridges. Think about the impact of the building on his audience: the height and scale, the large artworks in the lobby, the accomplishments that went into its construction. Craig told us that, for him, the building represents resilience, endurance, a fighting spirit. This is the setting of Craig's presentation. His job is to embrace that setting and inhabit it as fully as he can so that it can support and hold his story. Now think of the setting of your next presentation. Allow yourself to begin to inhabit that space mentally.

Often when we present, especially in a larger room, we tend to cling to the podium like a barnacle. There is a certain mythology about presentation and standing in the front of the room with little movement—as if that's the only way to hold everyone's attention! Break free of that restriction. The room is yours to use, and how you use it plays a role in how you connect with your audience. I tell my clients, "Presentation is about having choices." You may choose to stand at the podium, or you may decide to position yourself elsewhere, but make an intentional choice.

When it fits your story, you may walk to one corner with purpose. You may choose to stand against a window

on the opposite side of the room because you want to in-
vert the spatial relationships and have rear become front
and front become rear. You may opt to approach the audience. Every choice you make is about commanding attention. Attention is the currency of presentation.

IDENTIFY AND RELEASE
OBSTACLES TO LISTENING

Reapply the technique of identifying and releasing obstacles as you prepare for presentation. These include obstacles you might encounter in the room itself: Is it too hot
or cold? Too bright or dark? Is it ugly, and does that affect
our listening? You have to take in all potential obstacles
and release them so that you are not caught off guard by
your reactions to them when you begin to tell your story.
You also want to minimize listening obstacles for your
audience. Do what you need to address those obstacles
beforehand, such as opening a window or closing a shade
or reminding the person in charge of booking the room
that you have it reserved for a certain time.

Other obstacles to be aware of are the common fears
of public speaking and inherited beliefs about how presentations should look. If you reflect carefully on these, you'll
see that they involve a kind of preordained listening—
that is, "Audiences need to be entertained," or "Audiences

won't pay attention unless I start with a joke." By identifying and releasing these obstacles, you will cultivate the ability to start fresh and create a new listening and telling environment with your unique audience.

Presentation takes practice, experimentation, improvisation, and some courage. Presentation by nature should take you a little bit out of your comfort zone. You'll find that each step away from that zone is equally a step toward genuine and personal storytelling.

The steps of our method can be applied in a brief form on the day you will present:

1. When you wake up, remember your Why story? Why now?

2. Identify and release your obstacles to listening.

3. Remember your heritage to rouse your heart.

4. Practice the What happened? method with an unrelated event.

5. Review your story map and highlights.

6. Know your ending.

7. Walk into the room with natural confidence, and enjoy the connection you build with your audience.

CONNECT WITH YOUR AUDIENCE: A CASE STUDY

Connection always results from the Narativ method of listening and storytelling. How you utilize that connection is dictated by your Why story? Why now? In this case study of Narativ's work with a leading luxury brand in Paris, the connection aroused by honest storytelling transformed the legal department from transactional to proactive, and it became a true partner to the businesses of the company.

When we asked Sarah, the global general counsel, the question Why story? Why now?, she told us that the global legal team's purpose was to serve and support various business departments. It was critical for them to be seen as business partners within the company, but instead, they were often perceived as transactional and sometimes even as adversaries who were telling the businesses what they *couldn't* do due to laws and regulations.

As we listened to her Why story? Why now?, it became clear that there were stumbling blocks to communication within her team that were influencing their performance with the rest of the company. Team members came from the United States, France, England, Japan, South Korea, China, Russia, Panama, and other countries. Different cultural approaches to communication had led to miscommunication throughout the team that had interfered with their ability to explain laws and how they affected global operations. Since lawyers tend to think cerebrally and can be detached emotionally in their work, Sarah felt that personal storytelling would give them an experience of truly connecting with one another and create a foundation for improved collaboration through which they would better serve the business as a whole. Sarah wanted her team to understand that the way to connect with someone, in any context, is through story, and the heart.

During our first break in the training, Ken, a Japanese lawyer, said that he admired the trainer's ability to tell a touching and entertaining story. However, he confided that he was dreading being called upon to tell his own story. He said that public speaking was torture, and sharing stories was not something that people in his culture did, at least not professionally.

And yet, once he began to hear his colleagues' stories, the human side of their work was revealed: their day to day was to deal with fears and aspirations and pressure to achieve the goals of the company. Ken discovered his colleagues in a new way. His attitude toward them and toward himself shifted. Now he wanted to share his story because he related to the stories he was hearing.

Ken developed the following story in the workshop, which he presented to the entire global legal team:

I met my wife through a colleague and proposed to her on our first date. She told me I was forward and presumptuous. "You don't even know my last name." We married a year later and stayed married for a year. We argued about my smoking, her cleanliness obsession, my bachelor lifestyle, and her homebody nature. We were both heartbroken, but we didn't see how we could stay together. We divorced. Three years later, I asked her on a date. I proposed a second time, and she said yes. We are very much in love. Now I wear two rings to signify the two marriages. They're heavy, but I appreciate the weight.

There was not a dry eye in the house. Ken experienced firsthand the tremendous feeling of aliveness that accompanies the act of sharing a genuine story with a group of colleagues. He was struck by the number of people who thanked him and who wished that they could speak in front of an entire room the way he had. In everyone's eyes, Ken became a different person. They more clearly understood key aspects of his character and work ethic. He even became a different person to himself! What allowed that to happen was the fact that his colleagues had securely held out a wide-enough safety net of listening by suspending all judgments and opinions, listening only for what happened next. The listening and storytelling training they underwent created a self-reinforcing system: the deeper their listening, the deeper the storytelling, and thus the deeper the listening.

Ken also became a better listener to others now that he understood the value of supportive listening. His colleagues commented to us sometime after the workshop how impressed they were by his change and how they now felt his support in regional team meetings as a listener and capable presenter. They felt his camaraderie on the team in an entirely new way. This makes such a difference in communication and more so in advancing the mission of a particular team as a whole.

Ken and his colleagues continue to have a strong desire to pass the gift of listening on to others. Instead of feeling distant, removed, and competitive, they understand and receive pleasure from collaborating with other colleagues. Who wouldn't want to work in a mutually supportive environment where everyone was dedicated to the success of the team?

PRESENTATION

All the techniques we've discussed have one aim: to support you to tell a genuine and natural story in front of your audience. We want your body to remember your story when you stand in front of the room. Everything in preparation is about optimizing the conditions for that to happen. Following the steps of our method, personally getting to know its nuances through trial and error, making it yours to use—that's all preparation. Presentation is being present with your body and story onstage. As Charlie Parker famously said: "You've got to learn your instrument. Then, you practice, practice, practice. And then, when you finally get up there on the bandstand, forget all that and just wail."

We use the word *connection* a lot in this book, and it is what we're aiming for. When you remember your story in your body and tell it without notes or self-consciousness, your audience "relives" the story with you in heart and mind—that is *connection*. Our method prepares you. You have to be willing to go there.

Presentation Rules of Thumb

You have designated a time and space for listening and telling, be it a meeting, symposium, phone call, or sales presentation. You know how much time has been allocated and what percentage of that will be your story:

1. Before you begin speaking, connect to your body, establish your feet firmly on the ground, breathe naturally, and remember the story in your body. Scan the audience, resting your gaze occasionally on individuals.

2. Maintain eye contact with your audience. Throughout the presentation, establish individual eye contact with five or six people.

3. Slow down. If you talk too fast, you'll lose your listeners. This applies to most people: slow down the tempo even if it feels unnatural. This is where practice and preparation are crucial.

4. Pay attention to volume. If possible, present without a microphone. The absence of artificial amplification increases intimacy. But make sure that the people in the back row can hear you. If you're not sure, ask them: "Can you hear me?" This inspires confidence and creates an immediate connection with your audience. If you are using a microphone, make sure to test it before the presentation.

5. End with confidence and poise. Allow your story to conclude with a final standstill. Stay poised and keep eye contact with the audience as you allow the effect of the story to wash over them.

Learn from the example of Kai-Peter, who came to the United States to present a new German performance vehicle to an audience of journalists and car dealership managers. He excavated a story from childhood. His father was killed in World War II, so he lived with his grandparents. His grandfather, an avid car collector, regaled him with motoring stories, including one of watching the first production automobile drive through his town. The audience was moved and captivated. As he was drawing to a close, Kai-Peter looked at his watch, and he suddenly sped up his telling. Then the hotel staff came in with coffee. He was thrown off by this and hurried through the conclusion of his story—about driving the new model on a racetrack—as the audience turned their attention to the coffee break. What could Kai-Peter have done differently? He could have noticed the time, asked the audience to stay with him for the end of the story, and requested the hotel staff to return in five minutes. It takes chutzpah to do that, but it engenders tremendous confidence in your authority to be able to take charge of a situation.

Practice

Practice for your presentation. The ideal setting in which to first practice is in a pair, in a dialog between listener and teller. As we have discussed, these two are intertwined and rely upon each other. As much as this book lays out the principles and instructions of our method, we highly recommend that you practice it with a coworker, family member, or friend:

- Find a partner.

- Identify and release your obstacles to listening.

- Ask your listener to listen for What happened?

- Share feedback.

- Change roles and repeat.

By engaging in this process, you will feel the power of the connection with your partner. You'll understand that your story is an organism that's going to be iterated and reiterated. As people give you feedback and ask questions, perhaps because things won't be clear to them, you will adjust your story, and it will continue to evolve. In the midst of telling, new memories may bubble up to the surface as your body recalls experiences. You can collect those and integrate them into future iterations of the story.

Most important, I urge you never to learn your story by heart because that will impede your in-the-moment creativity and capacity to present with genuineness. Once you've trained your brain and body to tell the story and you've prepared your listening environment to the best of your ability, there is nothing more to remember. There is no need for notes. You and your story are enough.

Now share your story. Connect with your body. Connect with your story. Connect with your listeners (Figure 7.1).

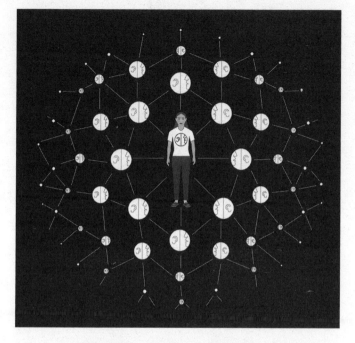

FIGURE 7.1 **A World Connected by Listening and Telling**

Keep listening to the stories that are told to you as a result of telling yours. Let those stories permeate the fabric of your being and that of your business. Enjoy the ripple effect that you will experience as a result of sharing your stories with others and listening to theirs. Allow yourself and your communication to be transformed.

EPILOGUE

··

Throughout this book, you've read how businesses have used listening and storytelling to reshape their communication. You've seen how our method lays out a highly structured communication pathway with plenty of room for invention. And you've understood that connection demands that we use the personal to imbue business communication with genuine connective power.

Without fail, the mindset of the leaders who've come to work with Narativ is one of openness and vision. They are open to creative alternatives to communication stumbling blocks, and, whether through experience or intuition, storytelling resonates with them. They understand that connection depends on the creation of an environment, throughout the organization, in which obstacles to listening are regularly identified and released in order for stories to emerge. These stories become the DNA of the organization. Like DNA, stories make possible the inheritance of core values while keeping open the possibility of evolution and adaptation as time and conditions change. Visionary leaders harvest them for insights, utilize them to share knowledge, and employ them to foster genuine connection.

Transformation isn't easy or simple. Old habits die hard. At first, identifying and releasing obstacles to listening at the beginning of a meeting might feel awkward and like a waste of time. Likewise practicing the What happened? method may seem unnatural and counterintuitive. Relying on jargon and well-worn assumptions may appear to be the quickest way of cutting to the chase.

As is true of any advanced skill set, our method takes practice. With practice you'll develop an increase in self-awareness and the corresponding ability to notice cognitive and emotional listening obstacles when they arise. As team members grow in confidence using the method, they'll see how it streamlines communication by removing obstacles and helping the team to stay on point. We are all naturally drawn to open, connected communication, the type of communication the method revives, which becomes an indispensable asset to your company's human capital.

Changing behavior requires that we take a risk. Disrupting old patterns takes us out of our comfort zones.

Storytelling is not business as usual. Be bold. View this as an opportunity to exercise new communication practices that will transform your company from the inside out. Your ultimate audience, your clients, will benefit from this transformation as well.

NOTES

Introduction

1. Bernard Wood, "Human Evolution: Fifty Years After *Homo Habilis*," *Nature*, April 2, 2014, pp. 31–33.
2. Indeed, it is estimated that 65 percent of our time is spent in narrative. See Leo Widrich, "The Science of Storytelling: Why Telling a Story Is the Most Powerful Way to Activate Our Brains," December 2012, lifehacker.com.
3. See Mor Regev, Christopher J. Honey, Erez Simony, and Uri Hasson, "Selective and Invariant Neural Responses to Spoken and Written Narratives," *Journal of Neuroscience*, vol. 33, no. 40, October 2013, pp. 15978–15988; Jonathan Brennan, Yuval Nir, Uri Hasson, Rafael Malach, David J. Heeger, and Llina Pylkkänen, "Syntactic Structure Building in the Anterior Temporal Lobe During Natural Story Listening," *Brain & Language*, vol. 120, 2010, pp. 163–173; and Edward F. Pace-Schott, "Dreaming as a Story-Telling Instinct," *Frontiers in Psychology*, April 2013.

Chapter 2

1. An example of one study can be found here: Lucy Clarke-Billings, "Psychologists Warn Constant Email Notifications Are 'Toxic Source of Stress,'" *Telegraph*, January 2, 2016, http://www.telegraph.co.uk/news/2016/03/22/psychologists-warn-constant-email-notifications-are-toxic-source/.

Chapter 4

1. Barbara Myerhoff, *Number Our Days: A Triumph of Continuity and Culture Among Jewish Old People in an Urban Ghetto*, Touchstone/Simon & Schuster, New York, 1980.

Chapter 5

1. Steve Jobs commencement address at Stanford University, 2005, https://www.youtube.com/watch?v=VHWUCX6osgM.

INDEX

ABOUT THE AUTHOR

Murray Nossel, PhD, is the founder and director of Narativ. He sees every situation and every interaction as an opportunity for listening and storytelling, and he has taught storytelling for 25 years in more than 50 countries to more than 10,000 people. He believes that something personal and expressive lies deep within each of us—and that we all have a story to tell.

Nossel is on the teaching faculty of the Program of Narrative Medicine at Columbia University College of Physicians and Surgeons. He has taught storytelling at London Business School, City University of New York, The New School, Baruch College, Benjamin N. Cardozo School of Law, and the University of Maryland.

Narativ, the company Nossel cofounded, has worked with corporations as diverse as the Walt Disney Company, Time Warner, New York Habitat, UNICEF, Radisson Hotels, the Open Society Foundations, Birchbox, and Twitter.

Nossel has applied his listening and storytelling methodology in the theater and documentary filmmaking. *Two Men Talking*, a performance of his listening and storytelling method developed with Dr. Paul Browde, has been performed in the West End of London and Off-Broadway in New York. His film *Why Can't We Be a Family Again?* was nominated for a 2003 Academy Award. Nossel is currently producing and directing *Sala: The Letter Carrier*, a documentary film about a Holocaust survivor who resolutely chose not to tell her story until advanced age prompted her to speak.

Nossel is the founder and director of the World Mother Storytelling Project, a listening and storytelling movement that seeks to capture the stories of mothers around the world.

He lives with his partner, David Hoos, a physician, in New York City.

ABOUT NARATIV

Narativ, a communication consultancy with offices in New York and London, specializes in storytelling in a business context. Its consultants work with clients around the world, some of which include Prudential, Cigna, Time Warner, Disney, Twitter, Medium, Chanel, and Boehringer Ingelheim.

Narativ delivers its listening and storytelling method on-site in group workshops to audiences as large as 500 and as intimate as 12. These workshops improve connection and communication in teams while offering the many additional benefits explored in this book: deep listening, editorial thinking, audience awareness, and presentation skills.

Narativ offers online workshops for individuals who understand that a personal story plays an important role in defining one's history as well as one's career goals. In Origin Story workshops, participants have developed stories for use in podcasting, filmmaking, raising capital, business development, authorship, leadership, job applications, speaking engagements and presentations, and self-discovery.

Narativ utilizes the practices that lie at the heart of listening and telling—interviewing; story excavating, crafting, and presenting; recording; and impact analysis—to build training and knowledge-sharing programs for corporations. Clients have used this solution for on-boarding and sales preparedness training. They report that storytelling makes training content more memorable, relevant, and enjoyable.

Narativ resolutely believes that listening and story-telling are the optimal means to make a connection between two people and within teams, organizations, and society as a whole. Its vision has always been a world connected by listening and storytelling—a vision the world needs now more than ever.